DIALECTIC AND DIALOGUE

DIALECTIC AND DIALOGUE

Dmitri Nikulin

STANFORD UNIVERSITY PRESS

STANFORD, CALIFORNIA

Stanford University Press
Stanford, California

Printed in the United States of America on acid-free, archival-quality paper

Library of Congress Cataloging-in-Publication Data

Nikulin, D. V. (Dmitrii Vladimirovich)
    Dialectic and dialogue / Dmitri Nikulin.
        p.   cm.
    Includes bibliographical references and index.
    ISBN 978-0-8047-7015-6 (cloth : alk. paper)
    ISBN 978-0-8047-7016-3 (pbk : alk. paper)
    1. Dialectic.   2. Dialogue.   3. Philosophy, Ancient.   4. Philosophy,
Modern.   I. Title.
B105.D48N55   2010
110—dc22

                                                          2009042644

Contents

Acknowledgments   *vii*

Preface   *ix*

1   In the Beginning: Dialogue and Dialectic in Plato   1

2   Dialectic: *Via Antiqua*   23

3   Dialectic: *Via Moderna*   48

4   Dialogue: A Systematic Outlook   72

5   Dialogue: Interruption   95

6   Against Writing   119

   (Dialectical) Conclusion   153

Notes   *157*

Acknowledgments

I would like to thank William Desmond, Caryl Emerson, Eyjólfur Kjalar Emilsson, Rainer Forst, Manfred Frank, Lydia Goehr, Jens Halfwassen, Agnes Heller, Gregg Horowitz, Vittorio Hösle, Mikhail Iampolski, Robert Pippin, Mark Roche, and Arbogast Schmitt for their most enlightening dialogical and dialectical discussions, which helped this book take its final form. I am grateful to Duane Lacey and Erick Raphael Jiménez for their assistance in editing the manuscript, and to Emily-Jane Cohen, Sarah Crane Newman, and Tim Roberts at Stanford University Press for helping bring the book to publication. My gratitude further extends to the Alexander von Humboldt-Stiftung for the opportunity to work on the book at the Universities of Marburg and Tübingen, as well as to the Forschungskolleg of Frankfurt University in Bad Homburg. Finally, I want to thank my family—Alya, Alex, and Anastasiya—for their constant dialectical criticism and persistent dialogical feedback.

Preface

In conversation and dialogue with others, we discuss things that often seem trifling and insignificant, as well as things that appear important and even sublime. We *are*; we exist dialogically as beings that communicate with one another at the very moment that we are talking with others. But when we arrive at a conclusion by accepting some arguments and rejecting others, we are using an implicit method or set of methods of reasoning traditionally called dialectic. One can be in dialogue about dialectic; one can be in dialogue without using dialectic; and one can use dialectic outside of dialogue. The main questions discussed in this book are: What are dialogue and dialectic? And how are they related to one another? This is not, however, a systematic dialectical argument about dialectic; nor is it a historical reconstruction of dialectic and its development, where each historical stage might constitute a necessary step in a logical sequence of stages. It is also not a dialogue on dialogue. Rather, what follows is a story: one that discusses a tradition of philosophizing through dialogue while practicing dialectic. It is a story about the *birth of dialectic out of the spirit of dialogue*. Once dialectic is dissociated from dialogue, it understands (and misunderstands) itself in many different ways: as an art of conversing about any given thing, a universal method of correct reasoning, and even the completion of philosophy. However, all of these characterizations still seem to point toward the origin of dialectic as that of an unassuming simple conversation and oral dialogical exchange.

The consideration of dialectic and dialogue in their mutual relation is complicated by the fact that it is not ultimately clear where each of them belongs in the traditional division of philosophy, the sciences, and art. Despite its codification in literature and philosophy, dialogue is primarily live conversation. As such, it is spontaneous, which means that in dialogue every interlocutor is free. Therefore the outcome of a conversation can never be predicted in advance. Hence there is no science of dialogue. On the one hand, despite its being capable of self-description and self-reflection, dialogue is not a theory. Nor can there be a theory of dialogue, because dialogue can always be continued in a different way; that is, a person can express herself differently every time she is in dialogue. Yet despite dialogue's being both spontaneous and alive, it is always possible to discern traits of consistency within dialogue, but only *after* it has happened. On the other hand, dialogue also bears a resemblance to art. Indeed, dialogue requires conversational and communicative skills, and in this sense its consideration may belong to aesthetics. Moreover, dialogue embodies *aisthēsis* or the sense perception of a minimal corporeality, namely that of the voice. Thus dialogue can also be understood as the art of being—that is, the art of being together with other human beings or the art of being human. In the case of imitative, written dialogue, dialogue evolves into the dramatic literary art of presenting persons as characters, of asking the appropriate questions, and of making the proper dialogical move to and with another interlocutor. However, dialogue as oral conversation with the other *neither imitates nor produces anything.* Rather, dialogue allows interlocutors *to be* in communication with each other. Hence dialogue is not properly an art insofar as being only *is* and is not produced.

Dialectic comes about as the written record, fixation, and reflection of an initially unstructured and seemingly disorganized oral dialogical exchange. Yet dialectic emerges only after the act of a live oral dialogical event. As such, dialectic turns out to be the formalized and finalized product of the monoconscious disintegration of an original dialogue, which, despite its unsystematic nature and seeming lack of universality, is nevertheless a universal human phenomenon. Dialogue proceeds by means of mutual interruption, whereas dialectic moves by grappling with opposites, particularly at the moment of their alleged coincidence. Dialogue's purpose, which lies within itself, is to continue the activity of conversation and (well-)being with the other. Yet dialogue is not just *a* form of communication: dialogue constitutes the very *conditio humana*, because to be is to be in dialogue with one's dialogical partner(s). As such, dialogue is always meaningful and complete, even if it is not finalized at any moment.

The unpredictability of dialogue cannot but irritate the mind looking for a reliable method in search of regularities and propositional universal truths. Dialectic is suspicious of dialogue, in which dialectic sees too much chance and disorder. Although dialectic originates in dialogue, dialectic wants to liberate itself from its own origin, to forget it, obliterate the vestiges of the dialogical within itself, and thus become a strict science and method. Dialectic, then, intends to eradicate all accidentality from reasoning, or at least to channel dialogical conversation onto a course that would produce a proof or argument through joint deliberation. In this way, dialectic hopes to get rid of any dependence on the dialogical other, and thus it becomes monological. Dialectic builds itself up as a logical enterprise, as the art and method of constructing correct philosophical arguments in accordance with certain rules, and of choosing the right presuppositions as starting points.

In its various manifestations throughout history, dialectic takes many forms and assumes many faces, each unlike the other. A common ground for reasoning about dialectic in modernity—in Kant, Hegel, Schleiermacher, and Gadamer, all of whom take dialectic to be a major constituent in their inquiries—appears to be the understanding of dialectic as it is epitomized in Plato and Aristotle. Plato takes dialectic to be necessary for the destruction of incorrect theses. It is possible that a correct thesis is not reachable by a discursive dialectical procedure, but the correct thesis cannot be accepted as known or rationally justified without dialectical justification and argumentation. Dialectic grows out of simple, yet not simplistic, discussions about what and how things are, about those things with which we are constantly engaged in (making) the world, such as politics, love, and so on. As a method of rational justification, dialectic is based on spelling out the contradictions that arise in dialogical investigations of our common opinions about things. As the practice of questioning "what" a thing is by reference to opposites that occur as "yes" and "no" responses in dialogical exchange, dialectic is perhaps a kind of art. When Plato writes his dialogues, which both imitate and reconstruct real conversations, he is very much aware of the origin of dialectic within live dialogical exchange, but wants to elevate dialectic to a logically ordered and ordering way of conceiving the true in an ascent from primary assumptions to their undemonstrable grounds and the ultimate good. When Aristotle places dialectic within a logical system of elaborate and subtle distinctions, syllogisms, and tropes, he takes the project of dialectic to be an artificial systematization of his teacher's and predecessors' insights about correct thinking, which are already implicit within a seemingly casual and unsystematic dialogical conversation. Later philosophy, however, wants to eliminate altogether the haphazardness of conversational exchange by elaborating a sure art and method for coining universal, and not accidental, propositions.

Dialogue, too, assumes a variety of forms and appearances: among them, conversations in the streets and squares of Athens; guided school discussions; idle chat; symposia; Kant's after-dinner courteous table talk; salon *bon mot* conversation. There are an unlimited number of dialogic genres, and each can be renewed in an original way. In each of its forms, however, dialogue is always engaging and unpredictable yet non-contingent. The engagement is mutual because it occurs in conversation between interlocutors, and it is further reinforced by the untainted enjoyment of being with the other and the interlocutors' attending to each other, even though, at times, this may not be easy.

With its appearance in the works of Plato and his immediate predecessors, dialogue played a central role in both philosophy and literature, for at that time the two were not considered separate. Written dialogue became a favorite dramatic form for revealing not only universal ideas, but also unique human characters and irreversible events. Dialogical narrative can be understood as an alternative to dialectical restorations of prior events. This sort of narration is capable of weaving complex networks for understanding human relations by showing, sometimes indirectly through hints and associations, how things are or were, as it does in a detective novel, for instance. Literary artificial dialogue, then, combines features of dialectic with the art of narrative and uses methods of persuasion that are found in both.

In modern philosophy, however, dialogue is ousted by the advent of the Cartesian, self-centered, autonomous, and universal subject, who develops its dialectic of philosophical analysis as *the* method of correct reasoning. When this all-permeating author's ego ("subjectivity") attempts to suspend itself and thereby protect itself from itself and from its own intrusion into things, it mostly fails. Even if the author—who usurps the privileged position of reasoning and being able to see what is real as real—does not want to be *the* voice in an invented dialogue and constructed dialectical argument, he is still unable to commit literary suicide and get rid of himself either through fragmentation or by using various writing techniques, such as "automatic writing." For this reason, today (which is but the lengthy day of modernity) we seem to be experiencing a crisis of dialogue due to the solitariness of a single, self-isolating autonomous subject. Such solitude is often just loneliness among other lonely subjects, all of whom strive for, yet cannot achieve, a simple conversation with the other, for which they substitute an anonymous exchange of "no one's" opinions.

The fixed form of written dialogue occurs as an attempt to both artfully preserve and skillfully imitate oral dialogue. However, because dialogue is elusive and ever changing, it is difficult to pin it down in writing. Therefore one must invent artificial means and techniques, including that of written dialectical dialogue, in order to reproduce oral dialogue, thereby substituting for oral dialogue what is not oral dialogue. It is not by chance, then, that certain criticisms of writing began to occur at the same time as and together with the appearance of dialectic and written dialogue. One such critique that can be traced back to the enlightened Sophists (particularly Alcidamas) and Plato is that written speeches are similar to painted statues that mimic humans to an awe-inspiring degree, yet cannot talk back when asked a question, cannot defend themselves, and cannot be other than they are. Thus, even if the purpose of composing beautiful speeches where characters seem to talk to one another is to preserve their original discussions, imitative literary dialogue is still only an improper substitution for memory with a "reminder" that is incapable either of saving the things and conversations of the past, or of communicating them to the reader.

Perhaps one should not write, after all. Yet we do write, so perhaps it is just a (bad) habit. Writing is premeditated and fixed, and as such lacks both the flexibility of oral dialogue and the capacity to answer the question; neither can it grasp and hear all the subtleties and ramifications of the response. Although it is not possible for oral dialogue to follow all of the possible paths that are opened up with each new rejoinder in a discussion, oral dialogue is still capable of choosing *a* path. Even if it is not always the most appropriate choice, it is at least unique to the discussion. Written dialogue and its distillation into dialectic, on the contrary, have only one path that they have already realized and chosen to follow forever.

In the Beginning: Dialogue and Dialectic in Plato

Dialectic and Dialogue in Plato. In certain periods of antiquity, Plato and Demosthenes were considered *the* prose writers who set the standards of writing for later imitations and commentaries. That Demosthenes was a rhetorician and Plato a philosopher did not really matter in this regard, because literature had not yet been rigidly separated from philosophy or rhetoric, just as fiction had not yet been separated from strict (in terms of its logic) or persuasive (in its seductive beauty) speech.

As a writer, Plato composed dialogues, which in turn established written dialogue as the first *prosaic* literary genre accessible to the general public: Plato's dialogues were often published on the occasion of a large communal celebration in Athens. Before Plato, philosophers often wrote poems about nature to present their views (e.g., Parmenides' poem *Peri physeōs*), as they also did much later in antiquity (e.g., Lucretius' *De rerum natura*). Tragedy and comedy, which use dramatic dialogue, were also written in metric verse during Plato's lifetime. Dialogues were probably composed before Plato (tradition points to Zeno of Elea, or to a certain Alexamenus), but Plato was the first to use prosaic written dialogue systematically for the purposes of showing and constructing what is thought about a given thing through speech, moving from presuppositions to a conclusion and aided by the mutual effort of interlocutors.

Plato's logos, or speech, is unique in that it uses the achievements of

Socratic oral dialogical conversations in a constant and conscious opposition to Sophistic monological speeches, which establish their superiority not by demonstration or proof, but by persuasion. No doubt there is more of an affinity and similarity between the Socratic and Sophistic methods than their supporters assert, insofar as both belong to the first historically documented Enlightenment. Yet the Socratic claim is that there is something within us that is nevertheless independent of us and has its own logos, whereas the Sophistic claim in its Protagorean version is to "make the weakest speech the strongest," regardless of whether it is true or false by itself, since speech, logos, does not appear to possess anything in and of itself, independent of our intentions.[1]

In Plato we have a rare case where we can actually identify the beginning of a genre: that of dialogue, which is intimately bound to the practice of dialectic. Thus, in the beginning was Plato's logos of dialectic and dialogue. In what follows, I outline the main features of dialogue in Plato, and then trace dialogue's relationship with dialectic. My main claim regarding Plato's dialogical dialectic is that dialectic originally was an oral practice established in oral dialogue; written dialogue then appeared as an imitation of oral dialectic; and finally, written dialectic was distilled into a non-dialogical and universal method of reasoning.

Plato was the first writer to use dialectic systematically and to reflect on this usage and the limits of dialectic in his dialogues. In fact, he invented the very term "dialectic."[2] Plato's dialectic, however, is inseparable from the form in which he chooses to publicly present his deliberations—written dialogue. Plato's dialogues are complemented by a letter (the *Seventh Letter*), in which he describes the evolution of his political views and the failed attempts to embody them in the political constitution of Syracuse. The letter is *addressed to someone*; that is, it either presupposes an answer, or it could itself be an answer and therefore may be considered as the preserved part of an otherwise now lost epistolary dialogical exchange. Moreover, Plato appears to have been developing a set of more systematic teachings that were not published by him in written form and are known mostly from other testimonies (e.g., from Aristotle's *Physics*, the lecture "On the Good," referred to by Aristotle, Theophrastus, and the later tradition) and from some hints within the Platonic dialogues themselves.[3] These apparently systematic doctrines of a mathematical ontology are dialectical investigations reflecting oral dialogical discussions within the Academy.

Addressing various ethical, political, and theoretical problems, Plato refines the method of dialectic in his written dialogues as a philosophical appropriation of oral dialogical logos, embodied by Socrates' speaking with the people in the streets and squares of Athens. Through Plato, the genre of Socratic reasoning or discourse, *Sōkratikos logos*, soon becomes an established literary form. It is also used by many of Plato's contemporaries, including Aeschines and Antisthenes the Cynic, who themselves were disciples of Socrates and the latter of whom wrote dialogues against Plato.

Platonic Dialogue. The ancient aesthetic ideal is art as the imitation of being. Art is a skillful reproduction of the beautiful, which itself belongs to becoming. Spontaneous and alive, beautiful being escapes fixation in images and words. In this sense, Platonic dialogue is an art because it is an artful and artificial imitation of spontaneous Socratic discourse—that is, of an oral logos or conversation that follows its own logic instead of the one that an artist or a philosopher imposes on it. Attempting to grasp being or "what is" in conversation and thought, Plato develops an art of reasoning that strives to be more than an art—namely, a method of grasping the truth of a subject.

Plato thus deliberately uses Socratic dialogue both philosophically and dramatically, by dialogically rendering philosophy as dialectical and using dramatic effects that imitate oral discourse. As Bakhtin notices, among all of the genres, written dialogue is eventually reduced to either philosophical or dramatic dialogue, and yet neither of them is capable of retaining the multi-voiced polyphony of live dialogue. Of course, Plato did not invent dialectic as such. Socratic oral discourse is already *elenchic*; that is, it implies the proof of a point and the refutation of an opponent's claim by demonstrating the meaningfulness of its opposite. Plato's philosophical agenda consists, on the one hand, in rendering philosophy as a strict thinking that utilizes and constructs proofs and refutations. On the other hand, he strives to make philosophical reasoning appear true to life, as well as true to the very process of thinking and its "history," through the dramatic depiction of characters who interact in a commonly voiced discussion. For this reason, Plato confined the use of dialogue to two genres: the dialectical and the dramatic, and has produced unsurpassed examples of both, the influence of which has been enormous and enduring. Plato's published dialogues became a *sui generis* scripture for antiquity—*the* text to be learned from and commented on.

In an ancient testimony, when presenting the characters of his dialogues, Plato imitated the mimes of Sophron, a Sicilian poet.[4] This testimony is not well confirmed by other sources, and in general there is not a great deal known about ancient mime as a genre—its possible relation to a cult, or its connection with other literary genres of which we sometimes know only the names (e.g., hilarody or lysiody). Nevertheless, it appears that mimes were short dramatic pieces imitative of ordinary situations and characters in everyday language, which is stressed by their abundant use of proverbs. Mimes were written for at least two characters, and as such may have contributed to the presentation of alternating voices in the genre of dialogue.

The ambiguity of Plato's dialogues is deliberate and perhaps ironic, in that he refuses to opt univocally for either the dialectical or the dramatic. Why? Because Plato seems to recognize clearly the richness of oral discourse, with all its nuances and paths of reasoning that are possible at any moment; and yet, insofar as reasoning is discursive and thus can go only one way at a time, it cannot fully fit into a constructed dialogue. Hardly anyone else within the philosophical tradition has been capable of preserving the delicate balance between these two components of philosophy made real. Even contemporary philosophy does not withstand this temptation: whole traditions choose to present themselves, according to the standards of reasoning, as either strictly "scientific" (i.e., "analytical"), or "literary" (i.e., "Continental"). One might say, however, that bare argument, which lacks any context or historical background, is dry and thus empty of sense. Contrary to such argument, the sheer dramatic imitation of thinking is not binding for our thought, and in this sense is fictional and makes no claim of presenting things as they are.

Dialogue, Dialectic. A later Greek writer, Diogenes Laertius, who preserved stories and anecdotes about illustrious thinkers of the past, characterizes dialogue in Plato as follows: "A dialogue [*dialogos*] is a discourse, or speech [*logos*], consisting of questions and answers on a philosophical

or political subject, with due regard to the characters of the persons introduced and the choice of diction."[5] In its *form* Platonic dialogue is deliberately structured as a speech that imitates or reproduces in writing the
step-by-step reasoning in alternating rejoinders that is unwrapped in and
as an exchange between interlocutors. These rejoinders mostly contain
questions and answers, at least implicitly, except when Plato retells a myth
(e.g., in the *Republic, Timaeus, Politicus,* and *Critias*), which he disguises
as a humble attempt to illustrate a philosophical or political point without going further into speculative discussion. As questions, the rejoinders
mostly allow for a simple and unambiguous "yes" or "no" answer. They
thus refer to opposite positions, at least implicitly. The whole of the deliberation consists in questions and answers that move in terms of opposites.
Yet questions and answers cannot be separated because each question, insofar as it is a question, awaits an answer and presupposes it, even if the
answer is inconclusive or simply incorrect.

Thus the very form of philosophical dialogue is that of questions
and answers (in Greek, *erotetic* and *apocritic*), which tolerates the occasional monological incursion of a myth. The erotetic and apocritic form
is also the form of dialectical reasoning. Dialectic is an art or method of
reasoning that initially occurs in dialogue and has to clarify the essence
of a notion—that is, "what" a thing is. In this sense, Platonic dialogue,
as an exchange of rejoinders, is already dialectical in its form. Therefore
dialectic is originally and profoundly a dialogical enterprise of alternating
questions and answers that refer to opposites.

Dialogue and dialectic are also parallel in that both are capable of
ever further deepening one's understanding of a subject by considering it
from various sides, insofar as questioning and answering can always continue. But such an exchange cannot go on indefinitely, whereas live dialogue can; live dialogue cannot be finalized because it presents a personal
other that is not a thing and thus cannot be represented by a finite number
of features. Contrary to this, the subject matter of both Platonic dialogue
and dialectic is a *subject* whose "what" or essence can be (although is not
always) disclosed through a finite number of predicates and in a finite
number of steps of reasoning. Of course, once the problem or topic is identified in Platonic dialogue, it is not at all guaranteed that a discussion will
end with an agreement as its outcome, let alone with a firm conclusion.

As I said earlier, both Platonic dialogue and dialectic proceed in terms of opposites. Moving in and through opposites constantly opens up the possibility for contradiction, refutation (which is why Socratic dialogue is "elenchic," or refutational), opposition, and disagreement. Because Platonic dialogue presupposes disagreement in that interlocutors test and try to refute the other's opinion, such dialogue is inevitably *agonistic*, based on struggle and competition. The purpose of *agōn* is to win a dialectical competition by revealing a weakness and inconsistency in the other's claim by gaining the upper hand in the discussion, and by trying to persuade the other of the superiority of one's own argument. Live dialogue, on the contrary, is not dialectical, because it does not need to prove any claims (although it can do so accidentally); instead it allows for the expression of oneself, of one's personal other, together with and vis-à-vis the other person or dialogical other.

As we know from Xenophon's *Memorabilia*, Socratic dialogue can have *any* subject matter. Socrates seems to be equally eager to discuss the nature of beauty and raising horses, using the same technique of questioning and answering. Plato, however, who elevates Socrates to a philosophical saint—the guardian and protector of dialogue and dialectic—narrows the subject matter of his dialogues to questions of theoretical and practical philosophy. The former includes physics (discourse about nature), ontology (discourse about being), and metaphysics (which may be taken as the "leftovers of physics"). The latter includes ethics (which asks: "what is virtue?" and "can it be taught?") and politics (which asks: "what is justice?" and "how can it be implemented in the constitution of a (best) state?"). Still, since being, the good, and beauty are eventually identical for Plato, the separation between theoretical, practical, and productive ("aesthetic") philosophy is not yet as rigid and determined as it is in Aristotle and later philosophy.

Style. In Platonic dialogue as it is characterized by Diogenes Laertius, the *style* of a dialogue, its diction (*lexis*), must first of all correspond with its topic. Thus the narrative style of the "scientific myth" in the *Timaeus* differs from the enthusiastic and erotic style of speeches in the *Symposium*, which in turn is different from the didactic style of the *Laws*. However, the task of Platonic dialogue is more that of philosophically disclosing a thing or a notion than of dramatically presenting a person through individual stylistic peculiarities of his or her appearance or a uniquely recognizable voice. Hence, with rare exceptions, in a philosophical exchange the individual voices in Plato are often conventional and not as complex as they are in modern dramatic or novelistic dialogues, which are more concerned with the detailed and nuanced elaborations of each character's voice.

Above all, the dialogical style is, as I said above, prosaic.[6] In dialogue, only the rhythmic exchange of rejoinders is still poetic. Literary written dialogue must involve a consideration of the appropriateness and beauty of its expression, whereas the interlocutors in oral dialogue often use language casually and may not even speak in full sentences. They do not care as much about the embellishment of language and speech as they do about the expression of the other and their understanding of the other person, which is driven by a "dialogical eros" or the desire to speak to the other. Because of this, live dialogue is spontaneous and unpredictable, quick, and even sometimes perplexing. Hence, oral dialogue is led in prosaic—that is, non-metric and non-poetic—language. Indeed, poetry is an artful and artificial suspension of language to the point of its complete evaporation and transformation into non-discursive being, which is ordered through silence. Oral dialogue is discursive and keeps moving because it is the life of the mind, which does not stand still and does not keep quiet and always speaks to and from the other.

The Characters of Dialogue. Furthermore, the characters depicted in a written dialogue have to preserve the similarity and likelihood that would allow one to ask the proper questions and get the appropriate answers in a concrete dialogical situation. The Greek term for "character" is *prosōpon*, which means "mask," a facial appearance worn and assumed by an actor in order to represent a character. A mask, however, always looks the same; it rests on the face of a character and renders him schematic. The mask in a dramatic written dialogue, whether tragic or comic, represents from the outset a general idea embodied in a character. The character of live dialogue, on the contrary, must remove the petrified mask of his finalized and ready-to-wear identity, which is imposed on him by the anonymous opinion of *Das Man*. Each interlocutor must speak herself out in an unfinalizable variety of ways, doing so each time anew and in a new situation while still maintaining the never fully thematizable sameness of herself as her own other.

Plato does not remove the mask of a character and make him a unique person. This does not mean, however, that Platonic dialogue is merely a dry and charted representation of arguments that speak through the voices of sketch-like characters. In the *prooimion* to his dialogues, Plato usually pays more attention to introducing the speakers in their mutual reliance—that is, not as personal and recognizable voices, but in their interrelated entirety as it develops dialogically in order to elucidate a question that will be asked, a problem that will be posed, or a dialectical argument that will be developed. Some of Plato's dialogues represent an immediate exchange between characters, some are retold (the *Charmides*), and some (the *Symposium*) are carefully and dramatically crafted. Still, Plato's main task in a dialogue is to address and solve philosophical problems by using dialectical devices. This task inevitably schematizes the dialogical characters and makes them into dialecticians who are mostly impersonal theatrical masks that ask and answer questions.

Sometimes Plato introduces curious episodes, such as the hiccups of Aristophanes in the *Symposium* (185C–E), in order to make the development of a dialogue dramatically plausible.[7] Quite often, however, characters in a philosophical dialogue are reduced to nodding "yes" or "no" in response to a question. In other words, Plato cares more about the plausibility of the argument and dialogical situation in its entirety than he does about the plausibility of individual characters. This is, of course, understandable, because on the one hand Plato takes the transient in his characters—their respective individual features—as being incapable of speaking about the ideal notion or *eidos* sought in the exchange, and instead as constituting a hindrance to the characters' ability to grasp being. On the other hand, Plato is more interested in the arguments that he develops and delivers in dialogues, thus following the logic of argumentation and reasoning, than he is in the logic of a person's description or expression.

Literature and Art. As I have argued, written philosophy was considered literature in antiquity because formally it is written in prose; that is, it is not metric. Therefore written Platonic dialogue is also literature. But is literature art? This question does not seem to have an unambiguous answer. In antiquity, if art imitates nature or reality, literature definitely has features of art insofar as it imitates life. But literature, particularly philosophical dialogue, does not imitate life alone. On the one hand, literature also provides suggestions and arguments about how to improve the lives of people living together—politically by adopting laws, and individually by training themselves to be virtuous and good citizens. On the other hand, philosophical dialogue qua literature investigates the life of nature and the life of being without any hope of changing anything about either of them, because nature is what it is and what there is. Therefore literature is art insofar as it has an imitative component and imitates life (including the life of the mind) by depicting it. Literature also has a narrative component. If narration imitates the features of a person or a live dialogue, then it belongs to art qua imitation of life. However, narration does not belong to art if it is didactic (in which capacity it teaches us to become better citizens, particularly by learning history), rhetorical (by persuading listeners and readers), or investigative (making us learn by observing being, by reasoning, and through dialectic). In other words, literature may have features that distinguish it from art.

Why did Plato choose to write dialogues instead of composing treatises? In the end, considering a topic monologically from various perspectives, inventing stunning arguments, finding shrewd "sed contra" objections, and providing solid counterarguments might also be considered a dialogue. Yet this would not be a dialogue of persons and characters, but rather an exchange of abstract statements. There may be different reasons why Plato wrote dialogues—for example, as an attempt to refine and purify philosophical argumentation and deliberation from accidental features by distilling it into an obligatory argument. Besides, written dialogue may be considered an imitation of oral dialogue, which is always partial: one can always say more about any topic in a meaningful way. Such a dialogue is always implicitly connected to other dialogues, both those that have occurred and those that have not yet taken place. This connection is made possible by the constancy of one's expression in dialogue as an interlocutor. In this case, written dialogue is an attempt to reproduce the microcosm of a living conversation or logos.[8] Such an attempt, however, is inevitably flawed because a written fixation can never fully recreate oral speech, which is neither given as a whole nor ever fully finalized.

Platonic dialogue may also be considered an exercise in dialectical reasoning, in proofs and refutations, in tackling aporias, and in the codification of such efforts. For this purpose, a reproduced written dialogue is a particularly suitable medium because it advances as a continual exchange of rejoinders in the investigation of a subject through questions and answers that may be assigned to different speakers.

A dialogue may also be written for pedagogical purposes (e.g., the *Theages*, which was perhaps written by somebody close to Plato) in order to educate the young through participation in discussions and by providing memorable examples of proper reasoning. Indeed, critical dialectical reasoning was considered to be of the utmost importance for the citizens of a polis—a democratic political community where everyone should be able to defend their own views and persuade their fellow citizens through the force of their arguments.

Plato may also have chosen to write dialogues because a dialogue is an open speech, often with an inconclusive outcome. The lack of any clear conclusion might itself entice the reader to think through the problems that are raised in a dialogue as an invitation for further discussion. (This is the way Schleiermacher and the subsequent hermeneutical tradition read the Platonic dialogues.) Everyone is in the same position in relation to the text of a dialogue, which is open to further interpretations, some of which will arguably be better than others if they provide the guidelines for understanding and explaining a text.

Then again, Plato might have written inconclusive dialogues in order to tentatively present a doctrine that has not yet been fully elaborated, simply laying out a main idea for later development in other dialogues. As Charles Kahn argues, different Platonic dialogues realize various "schemata," rather than implementing a single doctrine.[9] These schemata, such as those of recollection or noetic vision, depend on the context of the discussion, and their representation varies according to changing circumstances. For this reason, each "scheme" allows for multiple accounts in different dialogues but not for an ultimate formulation. Hence if Plato accepts many different approaches and points of view on the same subject within one philosophy, but not in a fixed doctrine, then dialogue appears to be a particularly appropriate form for such a task.

Or, having thought about political philosophy throughout his life, Plato may have written dialogues in preparation for the establishment of an ultimately just political constitution (which in fact he tried to do several times in Sicily, without success). The fate and immortal glory of a lawgiver (of Solon) is far superior to that of a philosopher, because the lawgiver provides justice for all through action, whereas the philosopher provides "justice" for a few (his disciples) through thought. The only way that a philosopher can become equal to a lawgiver is by providing rationally justified laws. Clearly, dialogue is the best way to perform deliberation about the justness of laws accessible to a potentially wide circle of interlocutors. The minimal requirement for an ideal state would be that the worst injustice of Plato's life, the death of Socrates, which was probably his deepest trauma and impelled him to write, would never again be possible at the hands of the righteous and the pious.

Or finally, Plato may have chosen the genre of dialogue in order to retain the remarkable arguments of the illustrious thinkers of the past from their pitiful disappearance into the river, as well as some of their personal features and the unique intonations and overtones of their voices. That an argument can be saved from oblivion seems to be the case to a certain extent—for example, in the *Parmenides*, where Cephalus retells an old debate about the one and the many. However, it is never quite clear how much Plato himself adds to the discussion, to what extent he disguises his own thought as someone else's, or whether he simply invents a thought or appropriates another's thought as his own without mentioning the person's name (e.g., using the argument of Alcidamas without referring to him in the *Phaedrus*). That a person's uniqueness can be retained in the distinctness of his voice for those who have never met him is not at all evident in the Platonic dialogues, even in the case of the towering figure of Socrates. Later I will discuss the question whether written dialogue is capable of adequately preserving oral dialogue, being a genuine and enduring memory from which the original conversation and its living characters can be clearly heard, or whether written dialogue is just a faint reminder that inevitably remains a mere hint of conversations and people that are forever lost.

Socrates. Plato's dialogical characters mostly represent either historical figures or his contemporaries, although some are made up, such as Diotima in the *Symposium*.[10] The characters are often schematic and do not always appear as uniquely identifiable persons from the stylistic recognizability of their voices (particularly in the dialogues that are retold, where different voices are imitated by a single speaker). The dialogical characters are similar to actors wearing masks, although the masks of dialogical, dialectical heroes belong to those who ask questions and provide answers where the impersonal truth of what is being discussed is more important than personal features. There are, however, a few important exceptions—most notably Socrates.

Socrates is portrayed in his constant seriocomic inquisitive effort to know how things are, which he rarely establishes with ultimate persuasion and demonstrative certainty. Still, Socrates is elusive not only in his arguments, which make sense at every moment yet do not always make sense in the end; he is also elusive in his personality, which also seems to escape any final description or mask. The mask of the ugly yet ironical satyr that Socrates wears hides his own utter goodness—his real appearance—which is rarely seen and never accessible unless he himself chooses to remove his mask.[11]

Socrates appears as the main character in Plato's early "Socratic" dialogues and is the one around whom the whole of each discussion revolves. He is also present in the middle and later dialogues, where he often cedes his central role, in the *Timaeus* and the *Parmenides*, for example. In the late Platonic dialogues, which are often less dialectical and aporetic, Plato at times does not depict the process of the search for what a thing or a notion is, but rather lays out an argument for the justification of a thought that has been conceived in advance. From these late dialogues, such as the *Laws*, Socrates disappears completely.

Socrates is always different from what he seems to be: he appears to pretend to be somebody—not somebody else, but rather somebody who is not as he now appears. Being a great actor and impersonator, Socrates at times simply "retells" a story, humbly pretending to speak in someone else's voice without bringing anything of himself into the account, speaking only for another. (This occurs in dialogues from different periods, both in those that are retold and in the multi-voiced dialogues such as those in the *Euthydemus, Lysis, Charmides, Hippias maior, Protagoras*, and the *Republic*.) The Greek term for "pretension" is *eirōneia*, or "irony." Searching for wisdom and knowledge by asking questions of others, Socrates pretends (and is paradoxically sincere) that he does not know anything—that he only wants to know. Maybe he does not know anything and does not know what his ignorance means. Maybe he does know something but hides his knowledge. Maybe he has knowledge but does not know that he has it; or maybe he does not know that he has knowledge and knows that he does not know. But how can he claim ignorance if he knows that he is ignorant? Is it a "learned ignorance" about what cannot be expressed in an ordinary way and put within the subject/predicate framework? Or is it knowledge of *that* he does not know, but not of its *what*? In order to be able to answer all of these questions, at least for himself, Socrates must ask other people and also himself as the other (and the way to distance oneself from oneself is irony) together with others—that is, he must ask in dialogue.

Irony (which was a central concept in the Romantic interpretation of Plato, particularly in Schleiermacher, and also in Kierkegaard) is pretending to be somebody or something other than who or what you are. But if you do not know who you are, how can you pretend to be somebody else? And if you know who you are not, how do you know that, if you do not know who you are? In the case of Socrates, the irony lies in his pretending not to be as he appears to the others in dialogue, and thus it is to be other, to be capable of always asking about the same thing in a different way and about different things in the same way. Since Socrates all too often seems to entangle the question being discussed into a perplexing *aporia* rather than clarifying it, he inevitably irritates, or fools, others, not only his philosophical and political adversaries (the Sophists Euthydemus and Dionysodorus in the *Euthydemus*, Meletus in the *Apology*), but even his followers (Alcibiades in the *Symposium*). Here, irony is a suitable means for self-defense against irritation, frustration, and even envy on the part of other interlocutors.

One of the reasons why Plato wrote his Socratic dialogues is to preserve both an image of his venerated teacher (the dramatic) and his speeches (the dialectical), which otherwise would have been lost. It is, however, impossible to say how much of Socrates' oral speech is retained and how much of it has been added on to, corrected, or changed by Plato. For this reason, Plato's Socrates is rather a "reminder" of the other Socrates who remains inaccessible in his real otherness, his original logos, yet is always an erotic attraction—in an inescapable attempt to understand him—for everyone engaged in doing philosophy.

Socrates is the figure of the dialectician *par excellence* who is also equally *the* "dialogician." Because of his power to construct a correct argument, and more often to destroy an incorrect one, and because of his ironic and elusive wisdom (recognized by the oracle at Delphi but not by Socrates himself), Socrates is very difficult to deal with. Even his best and closest disciple finds that it is not easy to portray Socrates, who, like Proteus, was ever-changing yet remained the same, which may be why Plato eventually decided to suspend Socrates, as it were, and make room for others to speak and investigate and let them shine by themselves, even if only dimly, and not be eclipsed by the sun.

Aporetic Dialogue and Dialectic. Among the various kinds of dialogue and dialectic (such as didactic dialectic), aporetic dialogue, which ends in an apparent dead end or aporia, plays an important role. Aporetic dialogue, as Michael Frede argues, represents Socratic discourse as elenchic—refuting a proposed thesis by showing to the interlocutor that in the end the interlocutor himself has to accept a position that contradicts his own initial claim.[12] In order to prove the inconsistency of an original claim, however, Socrates himself does not have to commit to a thesis that is different from the one being advanced, or even to any thesis at all. Socratic refutation discloses a perplexing difficulty, an aporia, that seems incapable of resolution because of the contradiction that results from the dialogical exchange. Once the interlocutors recognize their inability to overcome the contradiction between the initial thesis and the conclusion they have reached, they have to abandon the claim and begin their conversation anew.

Aporetic dialogue is thus dialectical, and works as follows: the questioner asks a question, such as "what is *A* (justice, wisdom, friendship, love, temperance)?" To which the person who answers gives a response in the form of a thesis, which is a (tentative) definition of *A*: "*A* is *B*." For example, "temperance is minding one's own business" (*Charmides* 161B). It is then the questioner who is the dialectician, because he asks simple and possibly straightforward questions, trying to avoid linguistic and logical tricks—that is, the questions that would allow, and in fact implicitly suggest, a simple and unambiguous "yes" or "no" answer. By asking the appropriate questions and following the answers, the dialectician makes the one who answers recognize the absurdity of the initial claim because the conversation leads to the acknowledgment that, in fact, "*A* is *not B*," contrary to the original thesis, which is thus untenable and must be rejected. If *A is not* and *cannot be B*, one has to start anew with a different thesis, "*A is C*." And by the same procedure of asking questions it will most likely be shown that "*A* is *not C*" either, and that "*A* is not *D*," and so forth, applying the same dialectical procedure to different theses.

The job of the dialectician is thus elenchic (refutative) and negative insofar as it consists in asking questions that would disprove and destroy an incorrect thesis, which might (but should not necessarily) clear the way for the correct one. Since the task of the dialectician is to question and refute what is incorrect, and not to advance what is correct, Socrates is *the* dialectician because he does not have to know how and what things are (even if, perhaps, he often does), but only to *ask* the proper questions. Yet asking questions, it seems, does not presuppose positive knowledge or a clearly prescribed procedure of inquiry. Asking the right (dialectical) question is rather an *art* or a skill, of which Socrates indeed might not be able to give an account even if he manages to perform the art of questioning very well. Instead, he might only be able to hint at the inspiration and guidance of a divinity.

Since dialectical discussion often cannot come to a final and definite conclusion (e.g., in the *Lysis* or the *Charmides*), it remains to be seen whether, first, there is and can be a *correct definition* of a thing at all, one that is not dialectically refutable; and second, whether there is and can be a definitive *procedure* that would always lead to the correct definition of what a thing is. To the first question there is no apparent ultimate answer in Plato's early dialogues, and there are only hints in his later dialogues that need to be further interpreted in the context of the Platonic tradition. Socrates is often forced to recognize, with a mixture of sorrow, surprise, and regret, that he is utterly perplexed by his own dialogical and dialectical investigation and cannot come to a satisfactory conclusion.[13] The power of Socrates as a dialectician is *negative* and consists in making the interlocutor recognize that the thesis he is advancing is untenable because it is contradicted by the conclusions obtained as a result of Socrates' questioning and the subsequent unwrapping of a jointly voiced thought. Later, in the *Republic*, Plato portrays dialectic as capable of obtaining true knowledge and establishing science: dialectic becomes the pattern of strict reasoning. Yet even here Socrates admits at a certain point that dialectical interrogation surprisingly does not always result in firm knowledge.[14]

But why does Socrates so often have to recognize, toward the end of a discussion, that he did not arrive at a meaningful conclusion (the only conclusion being a lack thereof), and that he in fact doubts (perhaps ironically) that there can be any such conclusion?[15] Maybe, in line with his avowed ignorance, he himself does not know the answers and leaves the question open and undecided? Or perhaps Plato himself does not see any possible way out of the aporetic impasse to which the discussion brings the interlocutors? Or maybe there is a way out, yet Plato withholds it, inviting the readers to find it for themselves by thinking through the subject together and independently?

Some of the followers of Leo Strauss contend that Plato's dialogues often present intentionally fallacious arguments. Of course, Plato may purposefully depict a fallacious argument, as in his polemics against the Sophists. However, this does not mean that Plato hides the correct thesis or argument behind a fallacious one; for Plato is not only interested in showing how dialectical reason proceeds while reasoning or that it in fact often makes mistakes. He is perhaps even more interested in showing how a dialectically justified argument in a written and constructed dialogue is intended to point not at an implied yet hidden "esoteric" meaning, but rather at the very preconditions for establishing or rejecting a sound argument.

Platonic aporetic dialogue thus requires dialectic and cannot exist without it. It is no wonder, then, that dialectic developed within Platonic dialogue. The two coexist in a symbiosis whereby dialogue provides the opportunity for a question/answer exchange and dialectic leads that questioning toward the refutation of an incorrect thesis and the possibility of establishing a correct one. On the one hand, as the late ancient *Anonymous Prolegomena to the Platonic Philosophy* claims, dialogue imitates the art of dialectic.[16] Yet on the other hand, written Platonic dialogue itself imitates oral and spontaneous live dialogue, in which dialectical procedures are always already present and effectively used, although they are not always reflected on and recognized as dialectical.

As I said earlier, Platonic dialogue is both philosophical and dramatic. As philosophical, it can now also be described more precisely as *dialectical*, as dialogue that allows for, and by its very structure provokes, aporetic and elenchic investigation. As *dramatic*, it represents questioning through realistic characters, rather than just a set of abstract and justifiable propositions. Philosophical dialogue has to show not only what is true, but also why it is true and how the conclusion has been obtained—how the search for truth is conducted and the way in which the interlocutors proceed through twists and turns and dead ends. However, unlike in oral dialogue, in Platonic dialogues the characters are not fully independent of either the will of the author or the logic of dialectical reasoning. Not being autonomous, the characters of philosophical dialogue are not equal either: nobody can escape or withstand Socrates' ironic and seemingly elusive dialectical power, including the "professional dialecticians"—that is, the Sophists—and among them not even Protagoras.

Furthermore, in the process of dialectical reasoning, there is no symmetry between the one who asks and the one who replies. The dialectician is the one who asks questions, not the one who replies. As such, the questioner is not equal to the answerer, whose replies are for the most part already implied in and by the question. In live dialogue, interlocutors can always, and always do, change places: they ask, they reply, they talk *à tour de rôles*. A directed dialectical dialogue, on the contrary, does not welcome such multi-voiced dialogical exchange; it suppresses the independent and unique personalities of its dialogical characters, or at least subordinates them to the dialectical procession of the argument. When dialectic is systematically utilized and reflected on within a philosophical system and thereby emancipates itself from a skillfully written and constructed dialogue, dialogue as a written genre becomes obsolete and abandons philosophy.

Dialectic and Rhetoric. When Aristotle reports that Plato's predecessors the Pythagoreans did not practice dialectic,[17] he means that Plato was not the first to invent dialectic (Zeno of Elea had already developed a dialectical method to show that the many does not exist), but rather the first to *use* the Socratic method of questioning as a common technique in his published works. At the same time, Plato was also the first to *reflect on* that method, its range of application, its use, and its limitations. Such reflection, however, occurs within the process of discussion itself, which makes this sort of reflection particularly difficult. Plato uses dialectic in order to think about what dialectic is. Hence we find in his texts a number of discussions and accounts of dialectic according to its different aspects, the most extensive and systematic of which occurs in the seventh book of the *Republic*.[18] Yet even there we do not find an explicitly formulated "system" of dialectic.

The project of dialectic is developed by Plato not only as an elaboration and preservation, in writing, of his teacher's manner of oral disputation, but also in response to the Sophists, who developed practices of disputation that were often intended to demonstrate a contradiction in an initial claim. In particular, Plato opposes their conflation of philosophy and rhetoric, *philosophia* and *rhētorikē*, and instead tries to establish a clear distinction between the two.[19] The aim of dialectical philosophy is to produce a correct and logically structured speech about a subject in order to demonstrate to the interlocutors and listeners (the latter of whom cannot but become interlocutors as well, being involved in the dialogical discussion and its continuing interpretation) what that subject is. The aim of rhetoric is to produce a beautiful and seductive speech in order to persuade the listeners that the position being argued is and must be the case.

According to the project of dialectical philosophy, a claim is either right or wrong, depends on the thing itself, and (with some luck) should be unambiguously demonstrable by the means and methods of dialectic. According to the project of rhetoric, a claim is right if the speaker can make it appear strong and persuasive. Unlike the Sophistic contention that seeming correctness can be obtained by using various tricks, and thus by alienating, puzzling, perplexing, and eventually conquering and overcoming the other, dialectical discussion aims instead not at a personal victory, but at an interpersonal truth.

Dialectic is also meant to be a *therapy* for and purification of thinking that allows one to escape the loopholes of linguistic and logical ("Sophistic") traps. Dialectic thus helps its practitioners become "purified" of wrong opinions.[20] In particular, dialectic is meant to clarify what is said by using procedures that enable us to escape the pitfalls of seemingly accurate arguments that lead to perplexing and paradoxical ("against the common opinion") conclusions. Such is the seemingly correct yet ambiguous argument of the Sophist Dionysodorus in Plato's *Euthydemus*. Dionysodorus argues that if the good should be attained everywhere and gold is good, then gold, qua good, should be attained everywhere, particularly in one's own body. Moreover, a position appears to be equally provable by using fallacious arguments and ambiguous terms—not only a thesis, but also its opposite. Thus, since the father of one man is not the father of another, then that father is also *not* a father, and hence it seems that nobody has a father. On the other hand, since every father is a father, he appears to be the father of everyone, because, being a father, he is incapable of not being a father.[21] Dialectic, then, should first allow us to make the proper distinctions between the meanings of terms in logos, in speech and argument, in order to avoid ridiculous conclusions. And second, dialectic should help us to arrive at a clear and distinct understanding of what any particular thing or notion is.

The Sophistic Touch: "Distinguishing Names." In a different way, dialectic in Plato is also a response to the Sophists. Protagoras is known for having developed disputation or contention (*antilogia* or *antilogikē*) as a rhetorical exchange: the practice of discussion whereby equal argumentative force and success is obtained by opposing positions. Plato's dialectic, then, attempts to rethink the already existing practices of opposing arguments, *logoi* and *antilogiai*, without claiming that any conclusion can be proven except for the right one.[22]

That logos, which can be speech, argument, definition, reason, and reasoning, is the most precise instrument or *organon* of thinking but can also be treacherously vague, as is well known in antiquity. The clarification of the use and abuse of terms and the struggle against ambiguity seems to be a constitutive feature of the *via moderna*. The idea of a "modern way," however, belongs not only to the late Middle Ages and early modernity, but occurs already in ancient Sophistry, which is perhaps the first truly modern movement insofar as it stresses the autonomy of the inquisitive subject and the importance of procedure for the justification of a claim. Since a notion that is discussed dialectically is increasingly distinguished into subspecies and thereby multiplied, one must make univocal distinctions between terms in order to avoid perplexity and ambiguity.

Simply put, one must distinguish between the meanings of the same term in speech, because failing to do so can easily lead to confusion. Making the proper distinctions between meanings in speech and argument should allow for a distinct and clear (or at least clearer) understanding of what a thing is. Thus, straightforward and unambiguous syllogistic reasoning should be able to prevent unsound conclusions and poor judgments and therefore guarantee systematic and methodical access to the truth.

While logos can indeed be straightened out and clarified, it can also be perplexing and perplexed because a word can be *used* or *said* in many different ways. Since, as it seems, there is no method or a priori reason that might account for a term's precise and *finite* number of meanings—that is, for *all* of the meanings of a term—then one cannot tell in advance how a term or word will appear and what it will turn out to mean in the particular context of a dialogue or argument. Sophistic criticism exercises a great pressure on words and speech by trying to twist a term or argument into whatever the speaker wants and intends it to be. Hence Protagoras taught his disciples (for a fee, unlike Socrates, who never charged anybody for his conversations except in claiming their free time, which is the greatest asset of a free person) how to make the weakest speech and argument the most persuading and convincing.

One might say that dialectic is a program of saving the logos, the reason or argument, from manipulation and relativistic misuse. In particular, in order to produce a properly inquisitive dialectical speech and argument, one should avoid possible ambiguities, speaking instead as univocally and straightforwardly as possible. This approach is found in Aristotle and is implied in his "it is said in many ways" (*legetai pollakhōs*).[73] This means that, if we are to understand something, if we are to produce viable support for the point we are trying to establish and not be derailed by a Sophistic trick that blurs our reasoning, then we have to begin by making careful distinctions. In order to make sure that we apply our terms in the same way, we need to enumerate and possibly produce a full list of all the known and distinct uses of a word. Aristotle dedicates a special book in the *Metaphysics* (Book Δ), a *sui generis* philosophical dictionary, to describing the range of available meanings of philosophical terms. Thus "being" (*to on*) is used in four different ways, "nature" (*physis*) in six, and "substance" (*ousia*) in four, all of which are listed and properly defined.[24]

However, Aristotle was not the first to formulate a program of making careful distinctions between meanings. The immediate tradition ascribes the introduction of this project to Prodicus. Prodicus, an illustrious Sophist, was a rather enigmatic figure who went as a rhetorician to Athens around the beginning of the Peloponnesian War and stayed there for quite some time. We have only a small number of texts and fragments either by or concerning Prodicus. They are few in number even when compared with the relative paucity of textual evidence on other, older Sophists, such as Protagoras, Gorgias, and Hippias. Most significant are the fragments that bear testimony to the doctrine for which Prodicus was famous, namely, his teaching concerning the "rightness of names," or the correct use of names: one fragment comes from Aristotle, and eight are from Plato's dialogues.[25] Both Socrates (who heard Prodicus speak "thousands of times" and spoke highly of him) and Plato unambiguously supported the Prodican doctrine of "distinguishing names," which Plato employed throughout his own dialectical discussions in his dialogues.

Based on the textual evidence in Plato, we can say that Prodicus' teaching of the correct distinctions between names presupposes, quite simply, that one must try to trace all of the possible meanings of a word and the ways in which it is "said" (*legetai*) or used in language or logos. That "the name is different," as Aristotle tells us, means that it can be used in various ways in different contexts and thus can mean different things. For instance, "pleasure" for Prodicus may have three and "learning" two different meanings, and if we want to come to an acceptable conclusion regarding any one of them we need to apply the terms in the same way, and not differently.[26]

Thus the ability to know something and produce an argument that proceeds, step-by-step, from distinct univocal and clearly defined premises in a certain and correct order to a conclusion, presupposes making the appropriate distinctions concerning the terms that are involved in dialectical reasoning. The correct choice and use of names, then, is one of the primary tasks of dialectic. The program of "distinguishing names" presupposes studying logos as an argument embedded in language and paying attention to the proper distinctions between meanings, both between the multiple forms of one word and between different terms. This project is closely connected with the "project" of the Greek *Aufklärung* or Sophistic Enlightenment, which attempted to provide a demonstration or logos for any required point in order to make it philosophically significant and politically acceptable by rendering a particular argument as the most persuasive. Within the Enlightenment project, which no one can escape, it is important to show not only *what* is the case, but first and foremost *why* it is the case. Therefore Prodicus' appeal to carefully distinguishing between the different meanings of a term finds its fullest support not only among the Sophists and the rhetoricians, but also among their opponents in Socrates' oral dialectic, in Plato's written dialogic, and in Aristotle's formal logic. Prodicus' project thus became a commonly accepted and acceptable (and hence dissolved almost to the point of anonymity) requirement for argumentative reasoning, even if its purpose may have been understood very differently.

Laudable as it may be to make things explicit and render them clear and distinct by discerning their names and meanings, in the end such an approach may simply not be viable. Both Socrates and Plato recognize that, even if it is necessary to try to enumerate and exhaustively distinguish *all* the meanings of a word, it is still difficult, if at all possible, to do so. Indeed, nothing guarantees that we will be able to trace and identify all the ways in which a term is and can in principle be used, or that any given list, dictionary, or catalogue of meanings is and can be complete. In fact, if meanings refer to meaningful and true propositions, they cannot be extinguished in their entirety. Even if a term, a Prodican "name," has nothing to do with any semantic notion of truth, there is nevertheless another meaning that is always possible by deliberate and purposeful assignment, or by inventing a new, unexpected, and unpredicted situation (particularly in literature) in which the "name" can be employed differently. All uses come from logos, which, qua speech, is spontaneous and inventive. Logos addresses the other, and thus is implicitly dialogical. It does not hesitate to renew and renovate itself (often ironically and playfully), establishing, propagating, and multiplying previously unknown ways of thinking, thus ridding itself of the boredom and repetition of the familiar meanings of a term.

Each logos is thus always one *and* many. The program of "distinguishing names" is therefore polycentric rather than logocentric. It may even be considered "eccentric" (in the spirit of such practitioners as Prodicus and Socrates), insofar as every logos inevitably contains a plurality of meanings and each meaning points toward a central meaning that exists in virtue of a multiplicity of its peripheral "names," each of which is potentially the center of a constellation of novel meaning(s).

CHAPTER TWO

Dialectic: *Via Antiqua*

Dialectic, Once Again. Dialectical reasoning may, and often does, end with perplexing results, because there is no guarantee that a conclusion can be reached by the dialectical procedure itself. One must then begin anew, doing so again and again until the "what" of a thing is satisfactorily defined. At this point, bringing together everything that has been said about dialectic, about the context of its appearance, and its use, we may ask once again: What is dialectic for Plato?

Dialectic is a refined and sophisticated way of accessing the "what" of a thing or notion through definition by means of certain forms of reasoning. The dialectician shows and demonstrates what each thing is through a discursive, step-by-step process—not an act—of investigation that involves posing the appropriate (possibly unambiguous) questions and providing the correct answers, a process that originally occurs in dialogue with the other.

Saying *what* is right is an *act* of immediate intuitive grasping. But proving *why* something is right is a *process* of discursive dialectical investigation. Dialectic is thus a way of conversing that moves from one point to another in an orderly manner and provides a proof, demonstration, or rational argument—all of which are logos—as to what a thing is. The "what" of a thing is traditionally called its "essence," which contains in a "wrapped-up" form all of the thing's possible properties that in principle can be known and extracted from it. The purpose of dialectic is thus to know correctly the "what" of a thing but not its "is."

By questioning the other, the dialectician establishes communication with her. In other words, the dialectician cannot but be in dialogue, which is what developed into the genre of Platonic dialectical dialogue. Hence dialectic is the search for the correct logos, a definition that is justified in a dialogical conversation (*dialegesthai*) and is revealed through dialectical reasoning—not as an insight, but as what is worked out through a number of steps that can also include missteps and mistakes. Arriving at a commonly accepted conclusion presupposes a mutual agreement that follows the "logic" of both the subject being discussed and the discussion itself, and is not simply a consensus by the sheer force of rhetorical persuasion. This "logic" is implicit in dialectical and dialogical procedures, but it may also be thought about, revealed, and rendered explicit by dialectic itself. The "logic" of a thing appears in the process of providing its correct analytical definition. The "logic" of a discussion, however, is erotetic and apocritic, consisting of questions and answers. As I said earlier, dialectical reasoning proceeds by means of appropriate *questions* and straightforward, sincere, and simple *answers*. For Plato, then, the dialectician knows how to ask a question that will or can lead to an understanding of the "what" of a thing, *and* can anticipate the answer. It is by means of such common reasoning, as Diogenes Laertius says, that we "either refute or establish something by means of question and answer on the part of the interlocutors."[1]

Therefore dialectic presupposes reasoning in and by questions that ask, first, about the essence or the logos of a thing—what a thing is. Second, it presupposes asking questions to which there are straightforward and unambiguous "yes" or "no" answers; that is, dialectic advances through and by means of *opposites*. And third, dialectical reasoning presupposes that such questions be asked in a certain order, an order that follows the immanent logic of a thing as well as the logic of the dialogical interaction itself.

A famous example of Socrates' intimidating manner of dialectical questioning is found in Plato's *Meno*. Inquiring about virtue, Socrates shows the inconsistency of Meno's thesis that justice is virtue, because justice is *a* virtue, and there can be other virtues as well. Another notable case of dialectic occurs in the *Republic*, where Socrates and Glaucon are engaged in a dialogue that reproduces a dialectical discussion between themselves and imaginary opponents whom they impersonate in anticipation of the latter's possible objections and their own responses to those objections.[2]

Dialectical reasoning begins with an as yet unproven thesis about what a thing is, or rather seems to be: a claim that is provisionally agreed upon by the interlocutors as a starting point for their conversation. However, instead of coming to a conclusion at a certain point in the dialogue, Socratic oral dialectic, as it is presented in Plato's earlier dialogues, usually destroys the initial thesis. Such dialectic is aporetic and negative because it forces the interlocutors to recognize that the original description of a thing's essence was wrong and that they must now begin anew, doing so often without success.

Is it the case, then, that *any* thesis can eventually be dialectically refuted and rejected? If dialectic is solely negative, then indeed it only destroys false claims and does not establish true ones. At least that is how it seems from Socrates' ironic inconclusiveness: one can never say with certainty whether Socrates knows the answer to the question being asked or whether he simply asks questions and plays the fool at the same time, making dialectical questioning something of a carnival. In the *Euthyphro* (11D), Socrates calls himself an artist who is wise—that is, he excels in his art against his own will (*akōn sophos*)—because he often makes the argument advance in an unpredictable way, such that the discussion follows its own direction and proves itself to be either inconclusive or simply wrong and self-defeating, even if Socrates would like the argument to stand firm. In the *Symposium* (215C sqq.), Alcibiades suggests that the inner beauty of Socrates (who appears physically ugly) is divine, and so it may be that Socrates does indeed know what and how things really are. Socrates, however, insists on paradoxically knowing only that he knows nothing (in particular), which would mean that he does not have ready-made answers but only an insuperable curiosity about how things are and a desire to continue with his inquiries.

Dialectic and the Knowledge of Being. If any claim can be refuted by means of dialectic, then no knowledge is possible, and the dialectician is a skeptic who attempts a refutation of *any* given argument by showing that one can provide arguments both for and against a thesis that would appear equally strong and persuasive. Dialectic was understood as skeptical in the later Platonic Academy during the time of Carneades, where dialectic became a method of training in reasoning, proofs, and refutation. First, one would prove that *A* is *B*, but, as the second part of the exercise, one would prove that *A* is not *B*, and since *A* is neither *B* nor not *B*, which is proven with "equal force," *isosthenia* (the term appears later in Sextus), then nothing can really be proven or properly said about *A*.

Plato, however, hopes to escape a skeptical stance with respect to the use of dialectic. From the seemingly inconclusive Socratic dialectic of his earlier dialogues, which approaches its subject indefinitely through conversation, Plato turns to a more convincing and conclusive dialectic in the *Republic*. Plato wants dialectic to be practiced as a *way*, one that leads, through appropriate steps of questioning, to the sought-after end of establishing what a thing is by itself, where "by itself" is independent of the dialectical manner or way of inquiry and the dialogical personas of the interlocutors. In his later dialogues, Plato reflects on dialectic and its appropriateness for such a task and shows how, by overcoming logical obstacles, dialectic moves toward knowing and demonstrating what a thing is—the truth of a thing. As such, dialectic must be able to help those engaged in a joint enterprise of asking and answering questions in order to know what and how things really are—that is, about *being*.

Dialectic is thus an explication of a certain kind of logos, namely that of speech, reason, and definition; such logos presupposes a discursive rational procedure, or a set of procedures, that show and justify the dialectical logos while aiming to achieve, as Plato says, pure and "unalloyed knowledge" (*akēratos epistēmē*). An important distinction for Plato is that between discursive reason or understanding (*dianoia*; Latin *ratio*) and non-discursive reason or intellect (*nous*; Latin *intellectus*), which was later carefully elaborated by Neoplatonists.[3] Discursive reason is logical thinking made present in speech and argumentation; it functions according to logical laws that are oriented toward the subject/predicate relation and preserve the law of non-contradiction. Non-discursive intellect, or *nous*, on the other hand, is capable of thinking a noetic form, *eidos*, in relation to the opposites of sameness and otherness that constitute each particular form and make it thinkable by itself and in its connection to, and contradistinction from, other forms.

Discursive reason advances or "runs" ("discursive" means "running," particularly in different directions and often without a clearly established preference) by starting with hypotheses or presuppositions and moving toward a conclusion through a number of ordered steps that follow certain rules and procedures of reasoning. The paradigmatic examples of such reasoning are proving a theorem in mathematics or establishing a sound argument in logic. Discursive reason unwraps itself gradually according to a certain logic such that the only conclusions that can be admitted are those that are clarified and justified in a succession of acceptable steps. Only conclusions that are reached in this way can be considered justified and proven, and thus a matter of knowledge. Such is the work of dialectic in particular sciences and philosophical dialogue: dialectical investigation begins with what interlocutors can agree on and then proceeds toward a conclusion by excluding impossibilities through reasoning with respect to opposites.[4] For Plato, the work of dialectic is thus the work of philosophy, which is why he often treats "dialectician" and "philosopher" as synonyms.

Discursivity, furthermore, signifies the inability to immediately obtain and have full knowledge of a thing or the thing itself in its fullness. Discursivity involves an inevitable partiality in thinking and the representation of any given thing and implies the *legetai pollakhōs* logical program. In a sense, discursivity is the *conditio humana*, which, if it cannot be altogether overcome, at least can be suspended by means of dialectic. Through dialectic one arrives at the right conclusion about a thing in such a way that all that has been previously discursively unwrapped is brought back together into the unity of a definition that now captures the "what" of a thing.

This is why Plato must also postulate the existence of a non-discursive intellect, or *nous*, that grasps the being of a thing, its "what" or "idea," in its entirety and by a single act of thinking. The intellect *is* what it thinks, and thus it knows a thing by being it, by being its non-physical "form." The form of a thing is inaccessible to either sense perception or imagination—that is, it cannot be sensed or represented. Such a form is not even accessible in its fullness and simplicity to discursive thinking, which can think of a form in only one of its aspects and always only partially (e.g., as a true proposition in a coherent theory). Dialectic thus provides a step-by-step argumentative restoration, a mediated and gradual gathering of the meaning of being, whose immediacy and simplicity is available only to the non-discursive intellect. As Proclus explains, the intellect contains in itself the dialectical powers and possibilities (*dynameis*) that it brings together into unity and completeness out of the partiality and multiplicity of discursive thinking. It is because being is undivided in its simplicity, and because the thinking of the intellect *is* being and is identical with its thought, that the non-discursive *nous* is capable of binding different methods and arguments together into one science.[5]

Understanding reason as essentially discursive becomes one of the keystones of modern science and philosophy. This claim is explicitly supported by Galileo, who, however, reserves discursivity for human reason alone, whereas non-discursive intellectual intuition is the mark of the divine intellect: "Our method proceeds with reasoning by steps from one conclusion to another, while His is one of simple intuition."[6]

Science as *scientia* or *epistēmē* is knowledge of both being and reason, of that which is the case *and* why it is the case. Hence it must act through reason by giving reasons, by rational justification, arguments, proofs, and refutations. Since the end of dialectic is knowledge, dialectic must be closely associated with the sciences. As Proclus comments on Plato, dialectic brings all the sciences together into one body of knowledge. But the sciences are primarily *mathematical* for Plato, because they deal with things that do not change over time—things that are not physical or bodily and hence are not immersed in the flux of becoming. Therefore the things studied by the sciences cannot be other than they are; nor can they be conceived of differently. Such are mathematical objects, which can be known from themselves with no apparent reference to physical, changing things. Therefore, in the last instance, dialectic must lead to the "one and whole mathematics,"[7] which is the knowledge of what and how things are, and cannot be otherwise.

Dialectic thus pertains to *all* of the sciences insofar as the dialectician must see and survey the sciences together in their unity. Because of this, in the *Republic* Plato places dialectic above the particular sciences and considers it to be their ultimate fulfillment, their "coping stone" (*thrigkhos*) and "bond of union" (*syndesmos*) because they are only able to present conclusions based on hypothetical premises that are grounded in the activity of discursive reasoning, which is overcome only in non-discursive thinking as the fulfillment and end of dialectic.

Overarching all of the sciences, dialectic must refer to a principle that is common to each, one that is pertinent to the subject matter of every science but is not itself the specific subject matter of any of them. In other words, dialectic must refer to being, and it must make possible the "science" or knowledge of being. Therefore, being must be better known and more clearly understood by means of dialectic than by the particular sciences, the latter of which dialectic uses as auxiliaries in order to elucidate being in and by thinking.[8] However, being can only be known dialectically in its polysemic essence or "what," and not in its simple existence or "is."

Dialectic and the Good. For Plato, everything both *is* and *is what it is* because it has a certain goodness, an appropriateness in its being what it is that thereby fits within the whole of the cosmos and beautiful arrangement of the world. If dialectic is to assist discursive thinking in defining what a thing is, it should also be of help in disclosing the good and distinguishing it from other notions or ideas. What, then, is the role of dialectic in knowing the good? First, dialectical reasoning must move through particular kinds of being that are "good-for," both in ethics and in politics. This should allow those who practice dialectic to become good. In this respect the task of dialectic is not only to demonstrate what being is, but also to conduce to well-being. This is why dialectic for Plato "implants and sows" the appropriate speeches, reasons, and arguments, or *logoi*, the pattern of which is mathematical reasoning that in turn may help those who participate in dialectical discussions to achieve well-being to the greatest extent possible for humans.[9]

However, the good *per se* for Plato is also the source of being, which does not properly belong to being. As such, the good itself is not being, or is "beyond" being. Only being is properly understandable within science, *epistēmē*, and is thinkable by *nous*. Therefore the good does not have a proper notion or definition. Or if it does, it can only be metaphorical or negative, in that the good *is not*: it is not anything in particular and it is not a specific good.[10] Dialectic, therefore, must lead not only to being, but also to what makes being what it is. Dialectic must ascend to the understanding of the first and non-hypothetical principle, to the good itself that is approached from the concrete sciences, which use hypotheses and presuppositions, hence advancing in terms of "if-then" arguments. When concrete scientific (mathematical and logical) truths are established, their hypotheses and presuppositions may be abandoned, so that the good, which does not need any presuppositions because it is itself groundless and is therefore possible in any hypothesis or presupposition, can be conceived without conception—that is, *not* as any particular thing or being.

Method and Methods. Platonic dialogical dialectic is meant not only to make correct judgments and justifiable claims, but also to be a systematic reflection on the very conditions of their possibility and fulfillment.[11] In other words, dialectic should be able to think about itself and dialectically establish its own essence. If sciences such as geometry, arithmetic, and astronomy have to submit their discoveries to dialectic, then dialectic itself must be the knowledge of the general principles that are common to all sciences: the pure—logical—form of knowledge.

The way of dialectic consists in a logic-oriented process of distinguishing and joining notions with reference to opposites. Dialectic should make it possible to know what each thing is, its essence and properties; and it should—negatively—even approach the good as such. Yet dialectic embraces a variety of concrete procedures, enclosing a number of different methods and logical devices. Such methods are considered independent of each other by both Plato and the later tradition that develops them. They are therefore mutually irreducible and cannot be subsumed under one another or under a single method. In this sense, Platonic dialectic still recognizes a whole *plurality* of methods, yet has no intention of becoming (as one might say today) the general methodology of all the sciences—that is, a single universal method, or *the* method to which much of contemporary philosophy would try to reduce itself.[12]

The method of elenchus, which is widely practiced by Socrates and dominates early Platonic dialogues, is a dialectical method of searching for (with the intention of reaching) the true definition of a thing and thereby its essence, by rejecting the wrong and inessential by means of a questioning that presupposes reference to opposites. In later dialogues, Plato's dialectical investigation of being moves in terms of the one and the many. In the *Sophist*, Plato presents dialectical knowledge in its capacity to distinguish things according to genera, in which one form is considered to be present in the many; the many as being embraced by one; one form as bound by the many in their entirety; and many forms as being by themselves, such that each one is completely separate from all of the others.[13] Such a "henological" dialectic, the dialectic of the one and the many, is developed primarily in the *Parmenides, Philebus, Sophist,* and *Republic,* but is also scattered throughout all of the major later dialogues and probably was also practiced in the oral discussions at the Academy.

Stressing the impact on knowledge of either the one or the many, Plato presents a dialectical method that implies two mutually related procedures: "collection," *synagōgē*; and "division," *diairesis.* The synoptic method of collection (for which the later Platonic tradition assimilates the Aristotelian term "analysis") is that of "bringing a dispersed plurality under a single form," or finding unity in the many.[14] The method of division, on the contrary, is that of "dividing into forms, following their natural articulation," and of descending to primary assumptions and premises by dividing genera into species or a whole into parts and then further into its indivisible constituents.[15] Collection means bringing various species under a superior genus, whereas the division of a genus is performed according to species. Both thus produce a "pyramid" of notions (although the starting point for diairesis is usually hypothetical, and each step in the division is rather arbitrary). Hence collection constitutes the way "from below"— that is, the way up from the many—and is thus opposed to division as the way "from above," which begins with the one.

Division and collection are the major but not the only dialectical devices. *Analysis* and *synthesis,* which also imply reference to the one and the many, play an important role in Plato.[16] These methods establish a relationship between elementary constituents (*stoikheia*) and a complex whole, the "models" for which are grammar that breaks speech into sentences, words, syllables, and letters, and mathematical knowledge, where a proposition is synthetically deduced from the starting principles (*arkhai*) or already established propositions and also analyzed back to them.

The later Platonic tradition (represented, for example, by Alcinous) also attempted to assimilate Aristotelian logical methods within Platonic methods of reasoning and searching for truth. Thus Alcinous mentions three further methods: definition, induction, and syllogistic.

Collection and definition study the nature of a thing in reference to its essence. Induction and syllogistic (which are systematically elaborated by Aristotle) study accidental properties: the former is an examination from the standpoint of individuals or particulars, the latter from the standpoint of universals. Within syllogistic, the elenchus is placed as a purely refutative method, whereas the demonstrative, apodictic, and syllogistic methods are associated with the Aristotelian syllogism, which is further divided into categorical and hypothetic.[17]

There are thus *many* different methods,[18] of which Plato does not bother to give an exhaustive classification—perhaps by reducing them to one single method and then showing a way of deducing all the methods from this single dialectical method. For Plato, every method is only *a* method, a tool for achieving a particular aim. And every workshop, including the dialectical one, has many different tools—as many as it needs—rather than one universal tool that the craftsman dialectician might use in the production of both masterpieces and failed or unfinished works. But most important, each dialectical method is a *logical* one. In the later philosophical tradition, which survived throughout the Middle Ages and even in the early modern university curriculum, dialectic was considered part of the trivium, along with grammar and rhetoric. In such a classification, dialectic, on the one hand, is opposed to the Pythagorean quadrivium of the exact mathematical sciences—geometry, arithmetic, astronomy, and music. On the other hand, dialectic, which is capable of proof, is distinguished from rhetoric, which is merely persuasive, and from grammar, which belongs to the proper arrangement of logos as speech. Dialectic, therefore, is practiced in order to study the formal properties of arguments irrespective of their content and to systematically arrange pure forms of thought, judgment, and reasoning. As such, dialectic becomes formal *logic*.[19]

The Art of Dialectic? Plato uses dialectic throughout his dialogues. But is it the universal method, the most general science, or the highest art? If dialectic is the "coping stone" of all the sciences, is it therefore itself a science? In antiquity, a science is defined primarily by its specific subject. Thus physics conceives of things that are mobile and exist by themselves; mathematics conceives of things that are immobile and do not exist by themselves; and first philosophy conceives of things that are immobile but do exist by themselves.[20] Yet dialectic is distinguished from the other sciences (arithmetic, geometry, astronomy, music) in that it ascends from the hypothetical premises of each science to non-hypothetical being and even to the good. Dialectic becomes the completion of all ("mathematical," i.e., strict) sciences, allotting to each one of them the capacity to act, judge, and think.[21] As such, dialectic is capable of considering *any* subject. Therefore, dialectic itself is not *a* science but assists by providing definite knowledge, science or *epistēmē*, of those things that cannot be otherwise—knowledge of how they are and what they are.

Plato considers dialectic to be the knowledge and science of being, a view held by later commentators.[22] As the knowledge of being, dialectic must be precise because its subject matter, being, is the most precise object of cognition and cannot be or be thought otherwise. But if dialectic is *the* science of the most general principles of things and thinking, it must be able to speak about everything and thus about nothing in particular, insofar as it provides the pure *form* for correct reasoning and conclusions. As such, again, dialectic must be pure logic. In antiquity, however, logic is mostly not considered a science, except by the Stoics, who consider it one of three constituent parts of philosophy. Instead, logic is a *tool* for thinking and drawing conclusions through arguments. Such a tool is also a method, a logical vehicle for systematically discussing any subject matter. Dialectic, then, turns out to be knowledge or science *par excellence*, as well as the method or tool of obtaining knowledge. For this reason, it becomes difficult to univocally classify dialectic within philosophy.

If dialectic is the knowledge of being and at the same time a method or a set of related logical methods for finding out what a thing is, then it would seem that dialectic is either *the* method for providing critical investigations and proofs of common principles that are valid for all the particular sciences, or the sum total of such logical methods. Yet if dialectic is the method of correct reasoning and proper questioning, it must determine which question should be asked and which turn or direction is appropriate at a particular moment in a discussion or investigation. Dialectic, however, does not prescribe how a discussion should proceed from the point at which it has arrived, or how to leave an unexpected dead end. Dialectic does not prescribe a route from beginning to end or from the premises that have been agreed upon to the acceptable conclusion. As such, dialectic neither allows for a closed "system" nor can be fully formalized (because of this, Plato prefers to present it through articulate dialogues) despite the later school's attempt to reduce dialectic to a method or a number of concrete methods. In this respect, ancient Platonic dialectic differs from the (unrealized) project of modern Cartesian and Leibnizian universal scientific method, or *mathesis universalis*.[23] This latter method was meant to provide clear, formal, and easy-to-use rules that were few in number and fit for solving *any* problem. It was meant to be *the* method that could be applied mechanically without much skill or deliberation by using an algorithm that could be univocally described and be applicable at all times without requiring an investigative effort. Thus, if dialectic is *the* method, it should be an empty method, a logic that describes forms of reasoning by abstracting them from, rather than prescribing them for, the concrete sciences.

Put otherwise, dialectic, on the one hand, is the science of being, of the essence of a thing, and even of the good. On the other hand, dialectic must also provide positive or negative methods (e.g., aporetic questioning that shows what a thing is not) that secure such knowledge. Because of this, again, in the Platonic dialogues there is no explicitly formulated single method for knowing being as the essence of a thing. In Plato's dialogues the use of these methods is shown through examples rather than through a systematic explanation. Speaking of dialectic, we face an aporia: Does dialectic uncover the essence of a thing, its "what," or does it only serve to justify that which one already knows? When Socrates in the *Meno* discovers a mathematical truth that he skillfully extracts from a boy who seems not to know that he knows it,[24] does Socrates already know this particular truth, or does he come to realize it together with his interlocutor as the discussion evolves? Correspondingly, are the dialectical methods ways of discovering new knowledge, or of justifying what is already known? If dialectic makes possible the discovery of something new or something that was unknown before the act of dialectical reasoning, then why do we not see the results of such discoveries in Plato's aporetic dialogues? Often, especially in his later dialogues, when Plato wants to communicate something as true, he does so without referring to dialectic; instead he either utilizes myth and asserts that it is a readily available conclusion (e.g., in the *Timaeus*) or employs a metaphor (e.g., in the *Republic*). The knowledge of being, even if possible, is not guaranteed through dialectical procedures; and if something is already known, then Socrates carefully avoids mentioning it and insists that he knows nothing, which means that if something is already known by extra-dialectical means, then it cannot be accepted as such until it is proven by dialectical questioning.

Dialectic is a way (which Plato takes to be *the* way consisting of a plurality of ways) of achieving rational justification—that is, of showing and demonstrating through discursive reason what is already known non-discursively by *nous*. Dialectic absorbs the concrete methods and logical procedures of particular (mathematical) sciences and in this way provides knowledge of being.

Dialectic is therefore the knowledge of both being and reason, of the reason *for* being, and is the knowledge that comes with reasoning about being. Since, however, the knowledge of what a thing is, its essence, can only be obtained at the end of dialectical reasoning and is possible but not guaranteed at the beginning, dialectic is therefore also the art of such knowledge, the skill of making and producing proofs. Hence dialectic has features of both science and art. Plato explicitly calls dialectic *an art, dialektikē tekhnē*.[25] What does this mean? In antiquity, art, or *tekhnē* (which also means "technology"), always establishes a relation to nature, or *physis*. Aristotle, a master of artful distinctions, also distinguishes between art as the skill of using (*khrōmenē*) and art as the skill of directing a production (*tēs poiētikēs hē arkhitektonikē*). These two aspects of art do not have to coincide (they can coincide, but only accidentally: thus a pianist uses a piano but cannot make it, whereas a piano maker produces a piano but cannot properly play it). Art either imitates nature or completes what nature is incapable of producing. In any event, the difference between the natural and the artificial lies in that what is natural has its purpose (as the form of a species) in itself, whereas the purpose of what is artificial comes from without, from its maker. Art involves a purposeful creation, which means that it is a production and implements a certain purpose: as art, it imitates what exists by itself. Therefore art, first and foremost, imitates nature: *hē tekhnē mimeitai tēn physin*.[26]

Hence, the better artist is the one who better imitates nature. Yet imitation is also a deception and an illusion insofar as it tells the truth by telling a lie. A famous anecdote preserved by Pliny recalls the story of a competition between two famous painters, Zeuxis and Parrhasius. The competition was won by Parrhasius because Zeuxis, having painted grapes, only tricked the birds that tried to pick them, whereas Parrhasius tricked a human, namely Zeuxis himself, by painting a curtain that Zeuxis demanded to be drawn away in order to show the picture behind it.[27]

Art, then, is contrary to nature, which art imitates or improves according to our purposeful intentions. Art should allow us to do something

that we cannot do naturally (e.g., travel on water, as in the art of navigation) and is thus anti-natural. However, dialectic for Plato does not have
to involve telling lies; on the contrary, it must tell and reveal the truth,
rather than improve it. Hence, as an art, dialectic must reproduce and
imitate the forms of thought and being by logos: in and through speech,
discursive reasoning, and logical argumentation and proof.

Art in antiquity represents the pure form, primarily in and as a beautiful body. Yet form (Plato recognizes a plurality of forms) is itself not
bodily and can only be thought. Therefore, every artful representation of a
form is necessarily a betrayal, even if that representation is itself necessary.
Every masterful representation is *not* a form but takes something *from*
form: truth, goodness, and beauty. As an art, dialectic represents form as
well, which for Plato is being according to how it is minimally embodied,
as it were, in a sequence of reasoning and conclusions that follow certain
logical rules. It is worth noting that science, which in antiquity is paradigmatically represented by geometry, considers objects that are even more
materially expressed and embodied in the geometrical materiality of the
imagination.[28]

Thus, if dialectic is an art, it is a different kind of art. As the art of
reasoning, discussion, and conversation, dialectic for Plato is the "royal
art":[29] it is the art of all arts. Art produces imitations of the living, the
beautiful, and the true. The "royal art" of dialectic, then, must produce
true and therefore beautiful conclusions about the essence of things and
show what they are beyond their appearances. As the universal art, dialectic must produce conclusions that also pertain to knowledge qua wisdom,
or *sophia*. The wise one, the *sophos*, is the one who is good at what he
or she does or produces—a wise weaver is one who produces beautiful
fabric; a wise astronomer is one who knows how the skies revolve. To be
wise *simpliciter* is to be good at anything that one does or makes, such as
producing beautiful speeches, signet rings, or anything else. The Sophists famously claimed (and were constantly ridiculed and questioned by
Socrates for doing so) to have been able to teach wisdom as such—that is,
excellence in any human activity—to anyone who would pay for it.

Art (*tekhnē*) in antiquity is commonly opposed to knowledge or science (*epistēmē*). As Aristotle tells us in Book VI of the *Nicomachean Ethics*,
art has to do with production and becoming, with those things that can
be or not be (i.e., that can be otherwise). Knowledge, on the contrary,

has to do with cognition and being, with those things that cannot not be (that cannot be otherwise). Plato, however, does not make a distinction between art and science in a systematic way, which may be the reason why his dialectic embraces the features of both strict knowledge (as the consummation of the sciences leading to the knowledge of being) and art (not as a prescribed set of procedures, but rather as the art of asking the right questions). Plato is aware of this ambiguity, which makes him reflect on the limits and uses of dialectic.

Moreover, art produces beautiful and true-to-life things that nevertheless are lifeless imitations or images, whereas science does not produce things but rather reveals and reflects on "what is," the being in things. Science discovers, rather than constructs, knowledge about things.

But knowledge is also opposed to art in that knowledge is reflective and concrete: to know means not only to have knowledge but also to know that you have knowledge (which Socrates claims not to have) and to know how to use it (as in the French *savoir*, which also means the ability to do something, as in *savoir faire*). Unlike science, art does not know the limits of its own application. Knowledge is thus not altogether dissociated from wisdom, because both knowledge and wisdom allow one to know what and how things are, as well as how to act in accordance with such knowledge.

Motivating an investigation by revealing the contradictions in particular claims and common opinions about things, by asking questions and replying to them while taking into account what has been agreed upon as a result of prior questioning, dialectic may be considered an art that produces not only positive, but also negative conclusions. In its negative capacity or power to reveal falsities, dialectic is destructive—in which aspect it also differs from art. (Being potentially destructive is the characteristic feature of art in modernity.) Socrates' art of negative dialectic thus presents a logos that suspends itself by straightening itself out step-by-step and painstakingly revealing to the interlocutors what is not the case.

But what is the relation between dialectic and dialogue in Plato? As a written oeuvre, Platonic dialogue is a work of art that belongs to literature (if literature is indeed an art). As a dialectical discourse about things that are intelligible, logical, natural, aesthetic, moral, and political, Platonic dialogue is therefore a work of argumentative reasoning and belongs to philosophy. As I have argued above, Platonic dialogue uses dialectic as a way of coming to understand the thing in question, of arriving at the definition of its essence, of what it is. As such, dialectic in Platonic dialogue can be used for the formal justification (of a logical and mathematical kind) of what is already known but is not yet formulated as true (and sometimes never is).

However, in order to reach and confirm its conclusions, dialectic, unlike dialogue, does not need the other of another person or of one's self. Dialogical logos is the logos of verbal exchange; hence it presupposes and needs a real other. Dialectical logos, however, is the immanent logos of correct and logical reasoning that embraces a whole variety of steps, methods, and procedures—yet it is solitary and anonymous. Insofar as dialectic moves discursively, it comes from dialogue and originally acts within it. Eventually, dialectic must break away from and overcome the inescapable partiality and inconclusiveness of dialogue, move beyond it to the universal impersonal knowledge of being, and thereby become non-dialogical. Platonic dialogue is therefore *monological*. "Monological dialogue" may seem like an oxymoron, yet Platonic dialogue is monological precisely because it is dialectical.

Since Platonic dialogue is a written imitation rather than a straight-forward reproduction of Socratic oral discourse (see Chapter 6), it also imitates the oral and spontaneous aspect of dialectic's not (yet) knowing in the process of reasoning and often going astray. Dialogue is similar to dialectic in that both presuppose the exact questions and answers that are appropriate at a particular point in a discussion. Dialogue may be dialectical insofar as it uses questions and answers that refer to opposites, but it may also be not dialectical insofar as it is expressive of a person. Dialogical speech implies the interaction of different, independent, mutually irreducible, and non-accidental voices in their exchange and non-coincidence. However, in Plato's aporetic dialogues, Socrates is an artful dialectician *par excellence* and rarely cedes the initiative to his interlocutors, whose rather dull function is to approve of the answers that are obviously implied in the questions. Because of this, Socrates' dialectical investigation is a monological interrogation, not of the other person but of the truth of the thing itself.

In a sense, Socrates may be thought of as an artist who often produces logos, a reasoning in its dialectical motion, but not a definitive conclusion or palpable result. (This is why Socrates, unlike the Sophists, does not sell his art.) This art of reasoning is unique because its product is alive and present at each moment in its entirety within dialogue, yet each time is only partially represented in discursive thought.

Dialectic as the Logic of the Plausible. The most significant rethinking of the role of dialectic in philosophy occurs in Aristotle, who dedicates his whole *Topics* to the study of the practical use of dialectic, which is now taken as autonomous and independent of the initial question-and-answer dialogical exchange. For Aristotle, dialectic is a specific—and rather technical—way of arguing that leads to a conclusion about any problem. As such, dialectic ceases to be the (or a) way of arriving at being and its understanding, as it is in Plato: for Aristotle, dialectic produces a dialectical syllogism, which is opposed to the strict proof of a conclusion, that is, to syllogistic proper. The reason for this is that, although Aristotle's dialectic also proceeds by not falling into contradiction and considering the opposites (taken as *contraria*, such as identical and different, similar and dissimilar), it does so beginning with merely *plausible*, or probable, premises—that is, the assumptions that may be agreed upon by the interlocutors at the beginning of a discussion.[30] As such, dialectic is distinguished from eristic, the art of confutation, which uses dialectical techniques in order to refute the interlocutor but that, as Aristotle explains, begins from premises that only *seem* to be plausible but in fact are not.[31]

Nevertheless, Aristotle attempts to appropriate a number of Platonic/ Socratic insights about dialectic for his own purposes. In a sense, Aristotle's study of dialectic is nothing other than a systematic investigation of the way dialectic functions in Plato's dialogues. Aristotle thus attempts to provide a general methodology that would be able to account for all of the particular instances in Plato's dialogical discussions of concrete problems (of justice, knowledge, courage, wisdom, and others).[32] Dialectic can be used for various purposes, such as exercise, oral dispute, and obtaining philosophical knowledge. The strength and success of dialectic lies, then, in its allowing one to carefully choose a subject for discussion, to discriminate between nuances in the usage of a notion (by "distinguishing names"), and to find differences and similarities between terms.

This new systematic and methodical dialectic differs not only from philosophy but also from sophistry: "Dialecticians and sophists wear the same appearance as the philosopher, for sophistry is wisdom in appearance only, and dialecticians discuss all subjects, and being is a subject common to them all, but clearly they discuss these concepts because they pertain to philosophy. . . . Dialectic treats as an exercise what philosophy tries to understand, and sophistry seems to be philosophy, but is not."[33] For Aristotle, the distinction between a dialectician and a philosopher is that the dialectician establishes the *order* of questions—the order of the steps in an argument—whereas the philosopher does not care about the order of questioning, but only about the correctness of the premises by which one can ascertain a conclusion. However, unlike Plato, Aristotle thinks that the philosopher does not need to be concerned with whether or not the other agrees with one's reasoning. According to this distinction, Socrates is not a philosopher for Aristotle, but a dialectician.

To further refine dialectic as a general technique of argumentation, Aristotle provides a careful distinction between various kinds of conclusions. There is, first of all, a *philosophema*, or proof and apodictic conclusion—a syllogism—which alone can provide knowledge. Second, there is an *epicheireme*, or dialectical conclusion from probable presuppositions. Third, there is a *sophism*, or eristic conclusion for the sake of gaining victory in a dispute at any cost, which in fact is an incorrect conclusion. And finally, there is an *aporema*, or dialectical conclusion, which implies a contradiction.[34]

Philosophy for Aristotle is thus opposed to both sophistry and dialectic in that philosophy is grounded in the activity of the intellect, *nous*, which conceives of arguments that are capable of understanding being as such, *ens per se, ens inquantum ens, to ontōs on, to on hēi on*. Dialectic, however, is based on a seemingly correct opinion, *doxa*, and considers (as does sophistry) only accidental properties.[35]

That dialectic cannot be the science of being for Aristotle seems clear from the following: if a dialectical statement is established by questions that imply a "yes" or "no" answer,[36] then such a statement cannot refer to the essence (the "what" of a thing) or to its existence. Why? Because to the question "does being exist?" one must always answer "yes" insofar as the notion of existence is tautologically implied in, and presupposed by, the very notion of being as such. Yet to the question "is this being?" one can still answer "no," depending on what one's concept of being is. However, the dialectical way of arguing cannot be used in either case: first, because the very concept of being does not refer to the merely probable or possible, but rather to an actual thing; and second, because in order to be able to say if and that something *is*, one must *already* implicitly refer to the notion of being as necessarily implying existence, since one must *already* be able to distinguish the existent from the non-existent. Therefore, the very possibility of making a meaningful reference to and asking about being excludes dialectical reasoning. This is another reason for opposing dialectic to philosophy: philosophy is not as concerned with arguments as it is with being, with *what* is and what *is*.

Besides, dialectic has much in common with rhetoric, insofar as neither one considers a particular subject matter, which normally defines a discipline; instead, both refer to opposing positions within their arguments. Yet the two are distinct: for Plato, rhetoric attempts to establish a plausible and persuasive conclusion, whereas dialectic aims at establishing a true one.[37] For Aristotle, in contradistinction to Plato, the difference between rhetoric and dialectic consists primarily in the structure of their syllogisms: unlike a dialectical syllogism, a rhetorical syllogism is an *enthymeme*, a syllogism with probable premises, one of which is omitted as evident (for the sake of shortening the argument and making it less burdensome), as something that is meant but not explicitly stated. A dialectical syllogism, on the contrary, is "complete" in that it explicitly lists all of its premises and tries to establish a reputable and correct opinion that will be acceptable to the interlocutors, whereas the "incomplete" syllogism or rhetorical enthymeme seeks the best available means of persuasion in each particular case.[38]

Dialectic, however, does not consider any particular kind of proposition. Instead, it speaks "about everything," which means that dialectic aids in considering the general principles of *all* the sciences insofar as it uses their results. But dialectic is not itself a science of general principles, because it does not consider primary, axiomatically true, self-evident, and general statements, such as "about every thing either an affirmation or a negation is true," and the like.[39]

When Aristotle distinguishes between theoretical, practical, and productive philosophy, he does not count dialectic as belonging to any one of them. Contrary to Plato, Aristotle opposes dialectic to philosophy because, unlike the genuine philosophical proof of a syllogism, a dialectical conclusion is based solely on opinion. The premises for a philosophical syllogism, which is the only sort of proof that provides knowledge, have to be self-evidently true, whereas dialectical premises are only probable. Nevertheless, even though it is different from and opposed to philosophy, dialectic for Aristotle can still be of much use to philosophy, namely, by displaying the possible inconsistencies in a philosophical position. And even if, logically construed, dialectic does not provide proper knowledge concerning the content of the subject it discusses, it may still show the *formal* consistency or inconsistency of its arguments by following the order of logical procedures that will lead to conclusions devoid of contradiction.[40]

Dialogical Dialectic and Logical Dialectic: Similarities and Differences. The seeming inability of dialogue to arrive at a definite conclusion stuns Socrates and his interlocutors. The dialogically shared speech that follows the twists and turns of an argumentative discussion in and by means of speech and reasoning seems to completely lose itself. As the discussion goes on, the initially clear term acquires a multiplicity of meanings that crawl off in all directions, and not a single one of them can be satisfactorily defined.

Plato thus faces the task of developing dialectic as a way of incorporating Socrates' seemingly idiosyncratic practice of talking to others, which is dialogical reasoning in questions and answers with reference to opposites. In this respect, dialectic may be considered an attempt to escape, overcome, and conquer the spontaneity and seeming arbitrariness of dialogical speech in its uncontrolled twists and turns and its almost uncontainable proliferation of different meanings for the same term. But dialectic is equally a response to the Sophists and their intention of producing persuasively strong, even if argumentatively flawed, speeches, thus substituting "what is" for "what seems to be": *pas être, paraître.*

Dialectic is presented by Socrates, according to Plato, as a discursive and argumentative *art* of reasoning that must be considered *the* art of finding and presenting logically provable, correct speeches about *any* subject. Dialectic therefore stands apart from particular philosophical disciplines. However, dialectic is not an overarching universal method for all the sciences because it uses many different methods, some of which are discussed by Plato (e.g., the method of diairesis in the *Statesman*); but they are not reduced to a single common denominator and are not deduced from a single method. As Plato himself tells us in the *Sophist*, dialectic considers the interactive yet mutually irreducible plurality of the one and the many in forms of thought or in ideas. Only the later Platonic tradition undertakes an attempt to classify various pluralistic dialectical methods (e.g., in the aforementioned *Prolegomena*), which it does, however, in a non-dialectical and rather unconvincing way.

The unique position of dialectic with reference to particular sciences is stressed by the Platonic and Stoic tripartite distinction of philosophy into the theoretical (the study of being), the practical (the study and practice of good actions), and the dialectical (the knowledge of logos, or reason, which includes the "reason-for" as well as reasoning itself, argumentation, and speech), which are otherwise known as the physical, the ethical, and the logical.[41] This uniqueness of dialectic can also be seen in that Aristotle separates it from philosophy as a whole and does not mention dialectic at all among the subdivisions of philosophy into theoretical, practical, and productive. Originating in dialogical conversation, dialectic is important and even necessary for philosophy, and yet it is not philosophy as such. Perhaps dialectic is pedagogically important as a propaedeutic to philosophy, or as philosophy's culmination on its way to being, which is nevertheless not philosophy proper; or perhaps dialectic is a *tool*, an "organ" of philosophy: a means to an end.

Both Plato and Aristotle agree that dialectic provides an indispensable instrument for reasoning that allows one to understand both *what* is the case (the essence of a thing) and *why* it is the case (the proof of the essence of a thing). But Plato and Aristotle substantially disagree about what dialectic is and how far its application extends. The difference between Plato and Aristotle (or rather the differences, if dialectic with its pluralistic methods is always at work in establishing the differences and similarities) is always important to note, because in the end any philosophical position might only be a variation on just two philosophical themes, those of Plato and Aristotle. If this were the case, every philosopher who subsequently discovered and established dialectic as a form of philosophizing would be either a Platonist or an Aristotelian.

Dialectic works differently in the two thinkers, and it understands itself differently by its own means. Platonic dialectic is embedded in a form of dialogue, which, however, becomes *artificial*—an art that imitates Socratic live dialectic in written form. Plato's dialectical "distinction of the forms" in the *Parmenides* and the *Sophist* is a distinction of the forms of being, of the ontological and epistemological patterns of things, rather than their classification into logical genera. Plato is ultimately interested in whether or not, and how, it is possible to think being. Thinking being *is* possible for him, and the way to do it is through the dialogical and dialectical logos, or argumentative and discursive reasoning. Such reasoning, however, must eventually be abandoned and is supposed to stop with the non-discursive thinking of being, which is itself being. This is the end of dialectic for Plato.

In this sense, Plato's dialectic becomes the ladder for thinking in its "ascent" to being, a ladder that, in the end, having led to the knowledge of being, becomes of no use and should be thrown away. To use Wittgenstein's metaphor, dialectic helps to release the fly from the bottle through the restrained motion of argumentative thinking to the freedom of understanding. Yet Plato's fly is released not into free flight, but rather into complete stillness and rest.

The Prodican program of what is "said (and used) in many ways," *legetai pollakhōs*, of distinguishing between the various meanings of a term and thus escaping polysemy, is differently realized in Aristotle and in Plato. The "rhetoricians" and the Sophists, including Prodicus himself, are concerned with names and their proper catalogue. Aristotle first proceeds by classifying and determining all of the "names" or meanings of a term as precisely as possible and then chooses the one he intends to work with most closely. Then, using various logical tools, procedures, and deductive techniques (e.g., the syllogism), he establishes argumentatively justified, proving, and proven knowledge of the correct meaning that refers to a real thing.

On the contrary, by distinguishing between various meanings, Plato intends to go further than Prodicus not only by using the correct name, but also by moving beyond the semantics of logos as language and argumentative thinking toward an ontology of the syntax of the forms. Plato is interested in discovering the thing itself, beyond the perplexing proliferation of meanings, and beyond the physical world with its flux of ever-moving and -changing things. For Plato, a "thing" is real, as neither logical nor physical, but only as thinkable. It is understandable in a momentary grasp of non-discursive, and thus "more than logical" thinking—in an *act* that is possible but does not follow with necessity from the discursive *process* of dialectical deliberation. In other words, Plato's project of dialectic presupposes asking not just about the univocal meaning of a term but about the precision of the thing itself.

Thus, for Plato dialectic has to lead, discursively, toward seeing the interconnection of the forms as the real things that are thinkable non-discursively. As such, dialectic differs from logic, which studies the relationships of words and their various meanings and roles within sentences and propositions.[42] Unlike Plato, Aristotle is concerned primarily with proper logical subdivisions of genera into species. Because of this, Aristotelian dialectic dissociates itself from its origin—that is, from dialogue. Unlike Plato's dialogical dialectic, Aristotle's logical dialectic is an *act* that embraces strict methods that are necessary for building knowledge. It is the art of constructing arguments dissociated both from their dialogical context and from the content of a thing, which is why such dialectic, being an exercise in the form of reasoning, still remains within what is plausible and thus can be of help in *any* science.

Hence Aristotle's monological and subject-oriented dialectic is a logical enterprise that employs all the available tools of formal logic and itself becomes a tool for any proper—formally correct—reasoning. In logic, a true syllogistic conclusion may follow from either true or false premises (although no true premises may yield a false conclusion). Aristotle's dialectic considers probable premises, which can be either true or false—it does not matter. What does matter is that both the form of reasoning and the conclusion be correct. Dialectic is thus about *form*. Yet this form is understood differently in Plato and Aristotle: for Plato, it is the form of being; for Aristotle, it is the form of logical argumentation. By using the logos of and in dialectic, Plato intends to move beyond it, whereas Aristotle stays within the immanence of argumentation, reasoning, discourse, and speech.

Dialectic and Beyond. Whether as dialogical questioning or as a set of related logical methods of reasoning, dialectic seeks not only to work and produce justifiable and sound arguments, but also to understand and reflect on itself. Defining itself by its own means is an essential moment in dialectic's own development and redefinition.

For the Stoics, dialectic and rhetoric are two parts of logic, which itself is one of the three constituents of philosophy, together with physics (theoretical philosophy) and ethics (practical philosophy).[43] On such an account, dialectic is a science "of the correct discussion of a subject by means of questions and answers." Dialectic, then, is an *ars disserendi*—a discipline that studies discourse and language, speech and its subdivisions, the construction of syllogistic proofs, different kinds of argumentation, the mental operations of the mind, the criterion of truth, grammatical and logical categories, and the like.[44] Dialectic, then, is not only intimately associated with logic as one of its parts, but is in fact identified with logic as a formal *tool* of reasoning that may be used for the consideration of *any* problem, whether in theoretical philosophy ("physics") or practical philosophy ("ethics"). Dialectic, then, conceives the correctness or incorrectness of logos in its various representations through reasoning and speech—universal formal logos. Such logos is everybody's and thus no one's, and hence utterly monological, mute, and opposed to dialogical discourse.

An attempt to further rethink dialectic in a way that would embrace it as both a logical and dialogical enterprise is undertaken by Plotinus, a great thinker of late antiquity, in his treatise *On Dialectic*. Following Plato, Plotinus stresses that dialectic is not philosophy *per se*, but rather its most "valuable part," because not only philosophy but also other sciences, such as physics and ethics, use dialectic. Dialectic, which is notably used by Plotinus for its own definition, enables us to speak "about everything by means of reasoning, logos, about what every thing is, how it differs from other things and what it has in common, and to what kind of things it belongs and where it stands among those things, and if it is, what it is, and how many existing things of this kind there are, and again how many are non-existent. It discusses," Plotinus continues, "what is good and what is not good, and the things that are considered under what is good and its opposite, and what is eternal and what not eternal, providing knowledge about everything, not opinion."[45]

Yet the most striking feature in Plotinus' reinterpretation of Platonic dialectic is that by employing, although in the end relinquishing, Platonic methods of division and analysis, dialectic makes it possible eventually to go beyond and *abandon* discursive logical thinking based on propositions and syllogisms. As such, dialectic must be distinguished from (Aristotelian) logic because dialectic does not provide knowledge *about* propositions and syllogisms, but in the last instance knows them nondiscursively, and thus not logically.

For a Platonist, such knowledge is the non-discursive knowledge of being or of the thinkable form of each thing, of its idea that, on the one hand, makes the thing what it is, and, on the other, makes it known— "seen" by the intellect (*nous*)—as what it is with all of its properties in their entirety. Dialectic is thus taken as knowing being by "ascending" to it from logical presuppositions and propositions, yet eventually leaving them behind. Such an ascent should mark the "end of the journey" toward the good. Dialectic, then, should allow for, and in fact necessitate, a complete withdrawal from and abandonment of any discursive logical thinking, which is useful during the journey itself but becomes useless once one arrives at the intelligible knowledge of "what is" and the good.[46]

Thus the project of Platonic dialectic appears to be rooted in the intelligible or the "noetic," which one has to "traverse" by using and then abandoning formal logic, which, in turn, is a "dianoetic" discursive activity. When the soul achieves "quietude," it becomes as though "illiterate" because it does not need to know any logical propositions or proofs as "letters," *grammata*, which are now utterly useless in their "grammar." Thinking becomes and remains a motionless activity of being and the non-discursive (and thus not dialogical and not logical, i.e., not dialectical) intellect. Non-discursive thinking thus abides in and around its origin, which is the good. However, the source of thought, the good, is itself neither being nor thinking, and as such it neither is nor can be known. Strictly speaking, the good *is not*; it "is" "beyond being." Hence non-discursive thinking, which uses dialectic in order to reject and overcome dialectic itself, does not properly have any origin or beginning. In the end, dialectic is without ultimate foundation, and hence is "anarchic."

CHAPTER THREE

Dialectic: *Via Moderna*

In later, especially modern, philosophy, dialectic is understood in accordance with new problems and tasks philosophy sets for itself. And yet the reflective self-transformation of dialectic is always performed deliberately in reference to ancient Greek tradition and oscillates between the poles established by Plato and Aristotle.

Art and Method(s). What does it mean that Platonic dialectic is the "most valuable part" of philosophy? Is dialectic first philosophy, or is it only *a* method for attaining being and an oblique look at the good? It is noteworthy that Plotinus, who emerges at the end and culmination of ancient philosophy, was still unsure about the status of dialectic, about what it is precisely: an art, a method, a skill, a useful tool that uses various logical devices, or a particular part of philosophy? Plotinus contends that dialectic is *not* just an instrument (*organon*) of philosophy, that it is not logic in the sense of an "organ" of correct and precise thinking. Indeed, logic deals with reasoning, speech, and its constituents, particularly with the meanings of sentences and single terms, whereas dialectic must conceive of being by using, yet ultimately abandoning, both argumentation and discursive reasoning. As such, dialectic for Plotinus turns out to be a *trained skill* (*hexis*, the term coined by Aristotle to characterize trained and trainable moral habituation or character), which uses correct and orderly discernment but ultimately leaves them behind.

As a skill of reasoning, dialectic must be able to define everything, yet it does not provide its own definition because then its task would be to overcome itself. Reflecting on itself by means of itself, dialectic thereby produces the metaphor of a *way*, a "method" of achieving the goal of reasoning, which is to attain knowledge of "what is."

However, the term "method" in antiquity does not have the same connotations that it has in modernity, where the idea of the universal method as a logical calculus of propositions becomes the guiding principle for investigation. Such a method should be based on an exhaustive enumeration of the steps of an argument, set in a precise logical order, that should be able to prove any true proposition, taking mathematics as a paradigmatic example of clarity, systematicity, and order of arrangement. This method is proposed by Descartes and Leibniz, but has its forerunners in Raimundus Lullus, Rudolph Agricola, and Petrus Ramus, all of whom take dialectic as a clearly defined logical method of investigation.

Ancient philosophy neither elaborates nor attempts to reduce itself to such an all-embracing universal method. Even if logic is an "organ" of philosophy, it must still embrace a number of connected yet independent methods and devices that consider the nature of an argument's premises (e.g., whether they are plausible or apodictic), and perhaps even the nature of the thing being considered (e.g., whether it is a mathematical or a physical object). In a sense, the ancient understanding of method is more pragmatic and sober: each method is only *a* method that allows one to attain a particular set of goals in considering a class of things or actions. Another task, or a different object, would require a different method. Furthermore, a method is a *way* of attaining certain goals; hence it is *a* method, *a* way. As "habituation," or a trained skill and way of reasoning, ancient dialectic resolutely abandons its birthplace of dialogue and turns into a kind of *reasoned art*, the practice of which should enable one to ascend to being and even obtain an impossible glimpse at the good beyond being.

If you are on a journey (and thinking *is* a journey, either as dialogue or as dialectic) from Trondheim to Rome, you have to follow a particular path. While there may be *many* different ways of reaching the end, any one of them will be different from the way that leads from Paris to Berlin, which has a different end. Each way, in a sense, is a method: the method for getting to the right place. Even etymologically, the Greek term *methodos* means "following after, (going or moving) along ('with') (*meta*) a way (*hodos*)" (for instance, in a hunt: Plato develops this metaphor in his *Sophist* and *Statesman*). Thus there may be *many* methods or ways according to the different tasks, and for each problem there may be different ways of solving it and arriving at the desired end.

The idea of *the* method is taken over by modern philosophy. Neo-Kantianism exemplifies this approach by suggesting that philosophy should not involve the consideration of being *per se*, which, as a substance or a "thing in itself," is not attainable by theoretical thinking and thus is not thinkable at all. On the contrary, according to Neo-Kantians (e.g., Rickert and Cassirer), philosophy must become a universal method and can be no more than a general methodology of knowledge. This idea is strongly criticized and opposed by many modern thinkers, such as Heidegger and Jonas, who themselves emerge within the tradition of rendering philosophy a method, yet nevertheless want to restore being as the simple (and thus hardly thinkable) origin of philosophy. In a different way, the criticism of treating philosophy as though it were a universal method is also shared by hermeneutics, which envisages a method for understanding textual historical reality as a method that wants, in fact, to escape being considered a strict method at all. The philosophy of science in the twentieth century also strives to become a sheer logical methodology for all the sciences, but even nowadays the sciences—mathematics, physics, chemistry, biology, linguistics—still use the idea of method in its ancient sense—that is, as a collection of many and often mutually irreducible and *different* methods for solving different and new kinds of problems. It is remarkable that, although distinct from science, art too invents and uses different methods and techniques for representation and concealment with various purposes and in various media. But even when the ideal of a single universal method is resolutely abandoned, its modern substitution and incomplete fulfillment, negative and without a clearly formulated set of rules, still tends to become a universal method in its own self-negation.

The Transcendental Turn. In the Middle Ages, dialectic construes itself as a logic fully dissociated from dialogue. Thus Abelard's *Dialectica* is a purely logical treatise. Dialectic understands itself as the logical ordering of an argument; by referring to opposites, it considers itself capable of answering any question, including dogmatic teachings based on revealed truths. Logic provides a correct, formal, and argumentative arrangement, a "reasoned calculus" or syllogism, from which, once the premises are accepted, a conclusion necessarily follows. ("All people are mortal . . . , etc." Alas.) As such, a syllogism represents clear and sure knowledge. However, nothing guarantees, first, that the premises themselves are true, and second, that the logician will actually be capable of discovering or establishing them together with a chain of reasoning that would lead to the sought-after (or sometimes unexpected) conclusion. Qua logic, dialectic is always fraught with the temptation of trying to establish a universal method that might uncover all possible truths from within reason alone.

Kant is usually considered a modern thinker and philosopher of the Enlightenment. Still, although he lived after Descartes, Kant might be understood as the last great scholastic thinker, because, on the one hand, unlike Descartes, Hobbes, Spinoza, Locke, Leibniz, Malebranche, and Berkley, Kant was not an amateur; he was still a professional philosopher employed at a university to teach curriculum courses, which was always the task of scholastic philosophers. On the other hand, even when Kant discusses modern themes, he does so in the traditional Aristotelian language, drawing much of his terminology from the scholastic tradition. However, when using scholastic terms, Kant almost always attempts to reconsider and appropriate them in order to solve specifically modern problems. In particular, he uses medieval dialectic to rethink it in his own—new—way.

Kant is aware of the temptation to reconsider dialectic as *the* method, as a universal logic of reason and reasoning that might yield the ultimate answers to the ultimate questions. He too faces the problem of where and how to locate dialectic in philosophy. While taking the scholastic Aristotelian dialectic as a formal logic that reveals errors in the form of its conclusions, irrespective of content, Kant needs to justify a new kind of dialectic, which he calls the transcendental dialectic, in order to reveal and criticize the very source and origin of propositions and notions whose objects cannot be given empirically, that is, do not pertain to any possible experience. And experience for Kant can only be constituted by the proper juxtaposition of sense-material with the forms according to which it is ordered by understanding, whereas the objects of reason lie outside the reach of understanding.

Transcendental dialectic thus emerges from the need to provide a proper critique of reason that is inclined to extend beyond the limits of possible experience and is inevitably captured by the "transcendental illusion." Such an illusion always arises (or rather, has always already arisen) when reason (*Vernunft*, the faculty of principles, a modern analogue of *nous*) improperly and unduly attempts to extend the use of pure understanding (*Verstand*, the capacity to subsume unordered sense-data under pure rational forms or categories, a modern analogue of *dianoia*) by using the categories in an extra-empirical way. Dialectic is thus a *logic of appearance* or a *logic of illusion*. The task of the new transcendental dialectic, then, is first and foremost to show, unveil, and unmask the illusion of an illicit judgment that oversteps the limits of possible experience, and at the same time to prevent the resulting deception.

Therefore the main task of transcendental dialectic is the critique of the rational illusion and unjustified claim of reason of achieving complete and absolute knowledge. Transcendental dialectic is thus meant to be a substitution for dialectic as the universal method of cognition and gaining knowledge about any subject from reason alone. For Kant, such knowledge is simply impossible and inaccessible to reason, because the pure notions or ideas of reason that define the use of the understanding in experience according to principles do not themselves describe any possible experience, but only the use of the categories of understanding in experience.[1]

Although Kant's turn toward a "new" transcendental dialectic arises from his own systematic project of critical philosophy, there are certain features of the "old" dialectic that he borrows from and shares with ancient and medieval thinkers. Thus the conclusions of the three rational disciplines are formulated in terms of opposites. (This is the case, for example, with the famous cosmological antinomies, although in making a distinction between opposing positions Kant argues that not all of them, particularly those involved in dialectical opposition, actually involve contradiction.)[2] Opposites are present to reason when it is caught by the transcendental illusion improperly applying its ideas. But reality *per se* is neither dialectical nor contradictory: contradictory statements (e.g., in rational cosmology) are due to a (wrong) presupposition that the world as an unconditioned whole can be an object of cognition for reason.

Transcendental dialectic allows for a systematic account and strict (although negative and critical) knowledge, which, however, remains impersonal and does not appear in or belong to personal (dialogical) exchange. Kant's dialectic is neither a science nor an art but a negative discipline of reason's critical self-purification and rational catharsis. It is the exercise of reason's self-suspicion and self-ostracism, of reason's caution against itself. As such, transcendental dialectic is a reflective *therapeutic* method that cures reason of illusion, improper functioning, and its own incorrect yet necessary misuse. Such an understanding of dialectic places it within philosophy as a *tool*, an *organon*, although this time as the instrument for reason's self-treatment and negative self-liberation.

The Impossible Dialectic of the Infinite: Coincidentia Oppositorum. The tendency to turn dialectic into a universal method is accompanied by uncertainty. As the "most valuable" part of philosophy and/or its universal instrument, dialectic must provide an indisputable conclusion about what any given thing is. Yet dialectic does not itself provide a clear hint as to how and when it should be used as a logical *organon*; nor does it indicate the possible limitations of such use. This uncertainty entices suspicion: even if dialectic ultimately points our reasoning to "what is," and directs reason toward and even beyond being, it may still be restricted in its use by the limits of reason itself. It is this suspicion that leads Kant to prudently claim that logic-oriented dialectic may be insufficient and inappropriate for reaching and understanding being, which may therefore need to be grasped differently, in a non-dialectical way.

This might mean that, through a number of steps of reasoning (which initially occur in dialogue with the other), dialectic can bring us close to being, but then fall short of providing an understanding of it. After an initial and indispensable course of dialectical reasoning, we may require an a-logical, non-dialectical jump (in)to being—from the discursive reasoning of logos to the non-discursive comprehension of *nous*. Such an understanding of the limits and limitations of dialectic might suggest that the two spheres of reason, discursive and non-discursive, which are differently understood yet present not only in Plato and Aristotle but also in Kant and Hegel (as *Verstand* and *Vernunft*), may have different laws of functioning. This would mean that if dialectic is oriented toward the use of opposites, it will function well within the discursive reasoning of logos, which respects the non-contradictory preservation of opposites, but will not work properly with the intellect that is supposedly non-discursive yet capable of grasping (the meaning of) being.

This is precisely the presupposition in Nicholas of Cusa, a Platonic Renaissance thinker. Chronologically preceding Kant, Cusanus was rediscovered by the Romantics during Hegel's time. Cusanus did not use the term "dialectic" in relation to his method, because he wanted to distance himself from the traditional scholastic notion of dialectic as a formal tool of logical reasoning. Hegel did not read Cusanus, but, as I will attempt to show, Hegel largely shared Cusanus' program based on the coincidence of opposites, which is essentially Platonic. Thus, in the philosophical history of dialectic, Cusanus in a sense comes after Kant.

Cusanus makes the "absolute maximum" the starting point of his philosophical consideration. The "absolute maximum," also considered the "not-other," that than which nothing greater can either be or be conceived, is at the same time the end-point of philosophy, both its goal and its completion. This absolute, the All, is the first being. It is the maximum of being. As such, it is infinite. Qua infinite, it is incomprehensible—one can only exercise a "learned ignorance" of it. Because only this infinite being properly *is*, everything else is limited and *is* from and because of the infinite. Because only this infinite being is, it is one, unique. Because it is one, it is simple—that is, it has no distinctions or divisions within itself. But since it embraces everything, it has everything *in* itself. In particular, it contains opposites within itself without being distinguished or split by them: opposites actually *coincide* in the infinite being, which embraces them without distinction. For this reason, actuality coincides with potentiality; hence the infinite is also "potential-actual" (*possest*). Similarly, the maximum is the minimum, and freedom is necessity. This infinite maximum embraces both an *A* and a not-*A* within itself.

Since the infinite maximum is one, nothing is opposite to it. In this respect, it is similar to substance in Aristotle, which has no opposite: substance mediates between opposites and is itself neutral with respect to opposition. The infinite is thus *above* opposition and opposites, which exist properly only for those things that allow for "more" or "less." The infinite, however, does not allow for degrees, precisely because it is the absolute maximum, and hence is always greater than anything else, including being. Nothing else properly *is*.

The infinite is incomprehensible. Thus, for Descartes one cannot know *what* the infinite is, only *that* it is. Therefore, it cannot be reached in any process, but rather only indefinitely approximated, the way a polygon approximates, but never coincides with, the circle into which it is inscribed. No mental process of thinking or reasoning, including logical dialectical reasoning, can help grasp the infinite. Therefore no philosophical method, including dialectic, can lead to an understanding of the maximum being. The infinite cannot be gone through, cannot be achieved by any number of steps; it cannot be "read."

The infinite, then, is the beginning of the finite, both of finite being and of the knowledge of finite things (in which respect early modern philosophers, such as Descartes and Newton, do not disagree with scholastic thinkers). To know what and how the finite is, how particular things are, we must somehow know or presuppose the infinite, and not vice versa. The infinite thus embraces all things, including opposites; everything is "wrapped" within it without any actual distinctions. In the maximum of being, all of the things and notions that are distinct in and for finite reason do actually coincide—the infinite straight line is both an infinite triangle and an infinite circle at the same time.[3]

Unlike potential infinity (e.g., that of the world, which is "privative" infinity in Cusanus and the "indefinite" in Descartes), actual infinity (which is "negative" infinity in Cusanus and the "infinite" in Descartes) is *not* in becoming (e.g., in making a magnitude bigger or smaller through addition or division), but *is* already and altogether a whole. However, such a "whole" cannot possibly be grasped by any of the available methods of thinking, including formal logic, just as it is impossible to understand how something can both be and not be, or be both *A* and not-*A* at the same time.

The infinite is thus incomprehensible to the finite mind, but it is also only for the finite mind that there exists a separation of opposites, and thus contradiction. Following the Platonic distinction between *dianoia* and *nous*, Cusanus also distinguishes between discursive reason and non-discursive intellect, each of which has its own sphere and laws that govern it. In constant and partial discursive thinking, we are exposed to an uncertainty when we have to choose the next step in our reasoning, which may or may not lead to a desired or sometimes unexpected conclusion. Here, reason or *ratio* is unavoidably bound by the laws of dialectic qua formal logic, primarily by Aristotle's supreme law of reason, the law of non-contradiction as it is formulated in Book Γ of the *Metaphysics*: "the same cannot at the same time be and not be in relation to the same and in the same respect."[4]

In (the rare moments of) thinking by the *intellectus*, we understand being in a single act. Here the intellect is supposedly not bound by the law of non-contradiction, because being is now considered without limits, infinite, and hence beyond opposites and distinctions. On the contrary, finite reason or *ratio* has to restore, in its discursivity, the "what is" of a thing through a step-by-step (not always successful) dialectical reconstruction in reference to opposites.

Cusanus' "project" of moving beyond the rational dialectic that preserves and respects opposites in attaining being is built on the properly ungraspable and hence rationally impossible notion of being as the absolute infinite. In this regard, medieval and modern Platonic thinkers differ from Plato himself, for whom being is a form and hence finite. However, they follow Plato and Plotinus in that opposites immediately and directly coincide in and for the intellect only (which is the sphere of being),[5] which is why dialectic qua logic has no ultimate authority here, unlike in the sphere of discursive thinking. Yet the Platonic position is equally different from Aristotle's understanding of being (as explained in Book Z of the *Metaphysics*). For Aristotle, being, as *ousia*, is present on the one hand as a finite thing or substance, which is a composite, *syntheton*, of matter and form. On the other hand, being for Aristotle is a form or *eidos*, the primary *ousia* that is concretely actualized in any existing thing. However, unlike the Platonic form, the Aristotelian form does not exist separately from the thing of which it is the form, so there is no need to recognize a transcendent sphere of eternal beings. Since, again, *ousia* itself does not have an opposite and is not opposed to anything, including another *ousia*, the Aristotelian world consists of opposition-neutral finite things, which are *studied* through but not *constituted* by the opposites, which themselves do not have a separate existence. Because of this, finite being is "logical" for Aristotle, and dialectic is an instrument for studying it.

In Aristotle's logic an opposite (*antikeimenon* or *antithesis* in Greek; *oppositum* in Latin) may be a *contrariety* (*enantion*; *contrarium*), which allows for mediation because it has an intermediate (*metaxy*) and is referable to an intermediate—that is, to an opposition-neutral thing as its substrate. Or, an opposite may be a *contradiction* (*antiphatikon* or *antiphasis*; *contradictio*), which has no intermediate and allows for no mediation, that is, it arises when opposites meet *immediately.*[6] In his philosophy, Aristotle looks for the mediating and opposition-free (natural) substrate (*hypokeimenon* or *substratum*) or substance (*ousia* or *substantia*). As a substrate, such a substance acts as a "third" that mediates between two opposites without, however, letting them be joined immediately. The immediate coincidence of opposites would amount to a violation of the law of non-contradiction, which for Aristotle is unthinkable and impossible and would destroy being and thinking. Hence opposites cannot exist as actual at the same time and should be thought of as contrarieties in relation to what is.[7]

However, Plato, whom Cusanus follows in this respect, rejects a third principle as an opposition-free substrate and thinks that the unthinkable—the coincidence of opposites—is possible. But such a coincidence, which cancels or suspends the principle of non-contradiction, is found only in non-discursive reason and is impossible for discursive thinking, for which all logical laws and principles remain valid.

The Platonic approach in attaining being and the beyond, which for Cusanus is being as the infinite, is thus to take opposites (such as same and other) as *contradictories*. To be sure, the Socratic aporetic dialectic always advances in finite terms of discursive reason and reasoning. As such, dialectic is not a koan-like enterprise; that is, it does not allow one to arrive at a non-discursive understanding of something by accepting the impossibility of a logically satisfactory response to a question that implicitly presupposes a contradiction, hence the coincidence of opposites. Dialectical navigation through opposites may not yield an answer, but if it does, the conclusion is reached discursively and the questioning itself does not violate the principle of non-contradiction.

According to an ancient anecdote, when Antisthenes the Cynic was about to read a speech saying that "contradiction does not exist" (*peri toy mē einai antilegein*), Plato asked: "How then can you write about it?" thus showing that the argument refutes itself.[8] In other words, discursive dialectical arguing that contradiction is impossible is performatively self-contradictory and thus itself *is* a contradiction.

The Dialectical Turn to Dialectical Logic. In his systematic attempt
at an all-embracing philosophical synthesis in modern philosophy, Hegel
adopts the Platonic thesis that opposites as *contradictories* coincide in and
for reason. This thesis reproduces Cusanus' claim that probably comes via
Bruno, although for his immediate discussion Hegel builds on Fichte's
Wissenschaftslehre (1794). At the same time, however, Hegel also embraces
the Aristotelian thesis that there is no rigid separation between the spheres
of being and becoming. In so doing, Hegel has to rethink the role and
method of dialectic in philosophy. An example of such dialectic occurs
in the very opening movement of Hegel's *Logic*, in a discussion of the
relationship between being and nothing: pure being is without any determination, and nothing is a simple equality with itself, void and without
content. Hence pure being and pure nothing are the same but equally also
absolutely different, and each one is inseparable from the other, so that
each one disappears in its opposite (*Gegenteil*). The truth of such opposites is their movement, which is becoming. Such movement, however, is
non-mediating between the opposites but signifies their difference, which
disappears at the very moment of being distinguished.[9]

In his *Encyclopedia*, Hegel distinguishes logical form according to
its three moments: (1) the abstract, or that of the understanding (*abstrakte,
verständige*); (2) the dialectical or negatively rational (*dialektische, negativ-
vernünftige*); and (3) the speculative or positively rational (*spekulative,
positiv-vernünftige*).[10] This division within logic is based on the distinction
between understanding and reason. Understanding (*Verstand*) conceives
determination (*Bestimmtheit*) and finite definitions as determinate, firmly
fixed and established in their separation and contradistinction from each
other. Reason (*Vernunft*), on the contrary, conceives a unity of distinct
and distinguished definitions in their mutual opposition. A completed
totality, speculative reason alone is capable of grasping the opposites in
their unity, which is inaccessible to understanding.

Hegel's first type of logic, the abstract, is bound by finite determinations that are considered definitive by the understanding. The understanding moves within the delimited either/or distinctions in which contradictories cannot coincide but are clearly distinguished and mutually
opposed. However, for Hegel every finite determination in itself is already
its own other: it potentially contains its contradictory within itself. The

coincidence of opposites is already latent in finite determinations but has to be actualized—thought—by reason through dialectic.

The concealed contradiction of the finite determinations is brought forward by and through dialectic, which releases the "positive power of contradiction." As such, dialectic is the negative moment, the movement of reason (*vernünftige Bewegung*) through which each seemingly separate determination and finite definiteness is sublated due to and from itself and becomes its other, its opposite.[11] Through dialectic each finite definition of the understanding thus moves into its opposite insofar as it contains within itself its own contradiction and hence its own negation. The inner contradictoriness of each finite determination is overcome in and by the sublation of the finite, whereby the apparent separation of thesis and antithesis is canceled or suspended by its entering into unity with its opposite in the resulting synthesis.

Dialectic for Hegel thus shows the one-sidedness of all the definitions of understanding, and it is through dialectic that each one, owing to its own nature, is set in motion and becomes its opposite, which is contradictory for the understanding but is reconciled as a unity within the speculative thinking of reason. As such, dialectic gives a *positive* result through a *negative* movement insofar as it shows only a negation of finite definitions and definite determinations through their immanent transition from themselves into their others and contradictory opposites—that is, their constantly turning "inside out."[12] For Hegel, it is not the understanding but reason alone in its speculative capacity that thinks opposite and contradictory definitions in their positive unity.

Dialectic thus constitutes the transition from the understanding to reason, from a potential, immediate coincidence of opposites to their actual unity in which the finite determinations are suspended—sublated—by being transformed into their contradictory opposites. Dialectic does not operate within the realm of discursive, abstract logical reason or understanding, but instead must lead to reason. In this capacity dialectic's role is similar to the one it plays in Plato's project, where dialectic operates with reference to opposites and leads to the apprehension of being—the forms in which reason conceives of the actual coincidence of opposites.

The coincidence of contradictory opposites, however, is inconceivable from the point of view of the understanding, which thinks about all things in finite terms and as clearly established in their mutual relations and separation. One needs to further postulate reason, which thinks of truth by embracing it non-discursively in its completion as and within a complete system of universal notions.[13] Only for reason does the impossible—Cusanus' *coincidentia oppositorum*—exist and become possible.[14]

This also means that Aristotle's fundamental law of thinking and being, the law of non-contradiction, remains valid for the understanding only but is invalid for reason, because reason is put in a position from which it is supposed to see, at a single glance, the totality of all the definitions in their concreteness and mutual transition beyond their apparent exclusion and isolation from one another. Hegel's dialectic thus leads to a suspension of the law of non-contradiction within reason, leaving non-contradiction suitable for understanding alone.

In this respect, Hegel is similar to Plotinus, for whom opposites actually coincide in the intellect or reason, but are kept separate within discursive logical thinking. Hegel, however, extends the sphere of logic to *both* understanding and reason, and the law of non-contradiction is suspended within one of the spheres of logic. With this suspension according to reason in its negative and dialectical as well as positive and speculative moments, the unity of opposites that are otherwise separate and isolated in the understanding remains utterly incomprehensible for finite and definite thinking. Hence reason, the speculative as such, for which the opposites do actually coincide and form a unity, is considered *mystical* insofar as it goes beyond the sphere of discursive understanding (*Enzyklopädie* §82). This "mystical" aspect, however, is not mysterious for Hegel, who seeks a rational clarification of the mystery of reason by means of dialectic.

A predictable objection has been raised by Popper: if the law of non-contradiction is violated, then assuming mutually contradictory premises and using the valid rules of deduction, one can deduce *anything*—any conclusion whatsoever or any number of conclusions in *any order*.[15] Such an objection, however, is beside the point here, because the law of non-contradiction is still valid for the understanding, which always proceeds in terms of clearly established finite definitions. Hegel's account of dialectic does not imply that self-contradictory theories would be true; in fact, he himself constantly criticizes other philosophical positions by showing their limitations, one-sidedness, and contradictoriness. The law of non-contradiction should be suspended within reason alone, which means that the sphere of application of this logical law is limited to argumentative understanding only. But reason for Hegel is not about demonstration and argumentation—it is about grasping truth in its totality, where seemingly opposite and contradictory statements are brought together through dialectic and are eventually reconciled and superseded.

Hegel takes his dialectic to be the "highest" and "true" dialectic, thus stressing its opposition to ancient and medieval dialectic in their inability to overcome or unite contradictory and mutually exclusive opposites. For Hegel, the shortcoming in previous accounts of dialectic based on the mutual exclusion of contradictories lies precisely in their failure to see the other as already implicit in each determinate statement and definition, which shifts into its opposite through dialectic. Hegel's dialectic, unknown to the ancients and alien to Kant, should be thought of, then, as "the activity of thinking thinking itself in itself."[16] As such, dialectic is the moving principle and instrument for constructing the systematic unity of truth within reason, which ignores the principle of non-contradiction and is based on the coincidence of opposites.

In his reception and interpretation of Platonic dialectic, Hegel shares Plato's fundamental presupposition that opposites are not and cannot be mediated in their interaction, or that one does not need to assume a neutral third as a substrate.[17] Yet Hegel's dialectic not only moves in terms of unmediated opposites, but also presupposes their actual coincidence. Although Hegel grants Plato the merit of developing a dialectic that moves in terms of logic alone—that is, in pure notions—he reproaches Plato for having elaborated and used primarily a *negative* dialectic, one that destroys and rejects incorrect claims. Socrates' elenchic dialectic is indeed negative insofar as it is aporetic. Moreover, unlike Hegelian dialectic, Plato's dialectic is unsystematic and fragmentary insofar as its argument often does not lead to a definite result. For the most part, negative dialectic does not establish a right thesis but rather refutes a wrong one, or does not lead to any conclusion at all. Such dialectic, however, is not self-reflective; it does not study itself by means of itself. When Plato claims in the *Republic* that dialectic must move upward and reach being by revealing the true forms in intellect or reason, his justification for this claim is neither derived from nor justified by means of dialectic. For Hegel, Plato's negative dialectic

only perplexes the mind by destroying a thesis, which results in every notion in Platonic dialectic being rigidly separated from every other, rather
than being deduced from within an all-encompassing rational system.[18]

Hegel takes his own dialectic to be negative too, but in a different
sense. His dialectic is negative in that it constitutes a necessary motion in
which determinations of understanding negate their finite definiteness.
Dialectic, then, opens up a space for reason to speculate about the finite
determinations in their (for Hegel, only apparently) contradictory unity.
As such, Hegelian dialectic is *productive*, insofar as it allows one to arrive
at the vision of a closed and complete system of speculative reason, which
is truth. This vision corrects, as it were, the initial myopia of not seeing
single, opposite determinations and distinguished definitions in their unity. Such dialectic is logical throughout, although the notion of logic is extended by Hegel to include both discursive and non-discursive thinking,
understanding *and* reason. Yet because reason "mystically" sees opposites
in their coincidence and unmediated unity, the law of non-contradiction
is suspended for reason in a way that surpasses the finite understanding.

Like Aristotle, Hegel makes dialectic a tool, an *organon*, of and for
philosophy. But unlike Aristotle, Hegel makes his dialectic a *universal*
tool, which becomes a necessary constituent of philosophy, its driving
force, a negatively productive method based on the *coincidentia oppositorum*. Dialectic becomes *the* method of philosophy, in which Hegel follows
the modern "project" of pursuing and developing one universal method
of cognition.

Paradoxically, one might see a fulfillment of the *coincidentia oppositorum* program in Derrida's attempt to overcome and cancel opposition
as such, to suspend any distinctions in thinking and textual interpretation, which is only possible when the opposites are thought to coincide.
However, such coincidence is impossible for finite thinking, and hence the
paradoxically negative self-suspending and self-canceling method, which
does not even want to be a method, does not sublate the opposites, as
Hegel's does, but rather annihilates them, promoting only an elusive other
without a same, such that the other itself cannot be thought at all.[19] One
might say that Derrida suspends the whole sphere of reason and assimilates its functions to that of the understanding, which therefore must—
but cannot—think opposites in their unity. In this sense, deconstruction
is based on the coincidence, indistinctness, and indifference of opposites

without their ultimate reconciliation and as such becomes the completion of dialectic through its ultimate self-denial.

Dialectical Logic and Dialogue: Hegel vs. Plato. But where is dialectic at work? According to Hegel, dialectic is the principle of rational movement whereby the concept immanently develops from within itself in its finite determinations. Engels interprets Hegel's understanding of dialectic as a claim that dialectic is universally applicable to movement and motion of *any* kind, to *all* phenomena of reality (nature, social life, history), in which every thing and every event is internally conflicted and bears its own negation, eventually changing into its opposite and other. However, this view of reality and of the applicability of dialectic is for the most part not shared by contemporary scientists and social scientists.

Yet the nature of physical, social, literary, and historical reality might not be dialectical and not subject to dialectical reasoning. As Charles Taylor suggests, the only meaningful use of dialectic is within an account of the goal-oriented activity of an individual or a group.[20] To understand such activity, then, is to understand how people conceive of themselves. Self-conception might contain self-negation, which brings with it a formulation of possibly contradictory goals or ways of achieving them. This means that dialectic appears important in understanding human communication and is to be found *in dialogue*, whether it is implicit or is explicitly formulated and used. As such, dialectic is at work in a dialogue with oneself or with the others in a group, in both spontaneous live and artificial dialogue (the latter being either literary or philosophical).

Hegel, however, criticizes the form of dialogue as incapable of representing and retaining pure thought in its inescapable dialectical motion, because dialogue portrays only accidental, concrete representations of thought, and not thoughts themselves.[21] Hegel recognizes that dialogue is *the* form of Platonic dialectic and philosophy, because only dialogue allows each interlocutor, as an active individual, to spell out their character and purpose and engage in a struggle that brings the action of thinking into real movement. That the interlocutors must disagree and struggle for their words is something that Hegel considers an advantage of dialogue, which displays a positive dialectical moment of productive tension. Such tension furthermore presupposes a dissensual relation between speakers, which alone enables them to interact properly, so that each one is capable of expressing or "spelling out" her particularity and of revealing what is general within herself. All these features, however, belong to dialogue as a complete and perfect *dramatic* form, which still does not make it the best form for philosophy.[22] At the same time, as Mark Roche observes, Hegel makes the workings of his own dialectic appear almost as a drama or a *Bildungsroman*, where the philosophical protagonist is the spirit that develops through "die Bewegung des Begriffs," or the dialectical motion of the concept.

Still, since dialogue only represents each individual in her uniqueness and individuality, dialogue is but an accidental, ever partial, and incomplete (i.e., unsystematic), form of philosophizing. Among the disadvantages of dialogue belongs, then, first, the utter arbitrariness of dialogue's unfolding, which for Hegel is not even a development, since this would presuppose an inner, immanent purpose. Indeed, one can never tell in advance where a conversation that depends on so many accidental circumstances might lead. Such indeterminacy often leaves the reader with the impression that, in the end, the discussion might equally as well have gone elsewhere, and that the conclusion—if there is a conclusion at all—could have been otherwise; in other words, the conclusion is not necessary but accidental. Second, the very form of dialogue contains heterogeneous elements. The properly philosophical presentation of being's unwrapping (which is thinkable and necessary) and representation (which is sensible, imaginary, and accidental) are mixed in dialogue in various ways that are utterly unpredictable, and that therefore do not belong to philosophy as a logical and systematic enterprise. A Platonic dialogue can always be or have been otherwise.

No wonder, then, that Hegel reproaches Plato for taking the good, the just, and the true as immediately presupposed and not dialectically deduced—that is, not resulting from a dialectical movement in which other categories (for Plato, ideas) would arise in their entirety as necessary and already implicitly contained in the finite terms and ever partial definitions discussed in dialogue.[23] Such a criticism is not at all surprising, since Hegel is primarily interested in dialectic as a universal method for building a system in which logical categories are deduced with rigid necessity, which dialogical dialectic appears not to possess, at least not explicitly. This is why dialogue is hardly ever mentioned and is never used by Hegel. In Hegel's entire corpus dialogue is referred to only five times, mostly in the lectures, and never in the *Logic*. Dialogue, in which opposites struggle as contrarieties but never coincide, is denied any potential of providing a systematic unwrapping or development of logic.

Philosophy for Hegel is a self-contained, all-embracing, and dialectically self-developing logical system. In such a system, the end and totality of truth conceived by reason as it thinks opposites in their alleged unity, is already immanent and is analytically presupposed in the distinct and partial determinations of understanding, and only needs to be historically and philosophically extracted, expressed, or embodied (in Hegel's own philosophy). Such a philosophy is revealed single-handedly, in a lone— and thus monological—lengthy reflection put into writing. This dialectical philosophy is thus anti-dialogical. It is presented in the mediating meditation of a single individual who must demonstrate the necessary and immanent development of notions from within themselves due to the *perpetuum mobile* of dialectic, and not in an occasional and accidental dialogical exchange.

While speaking about Solger (who together with other Romantics reintroduced dialogue into systematic philosophy in order to overcome the gap between philosophy and literature), Hegel notes that dialectic is the soul of dialogue.[24] This means that philosophical (fixed and written) dialogue originates in dialectic, which runs contrary to Plato's insight that dialectic is first established within spontaneous oral dialogue, often seemingly chaotic yet always organized in its exchange of rejoinders, questions, and answers by means of spoken logos. In Hegel, dialectic leads to the unthinkable yet necessary coincidence of opposites in unity. It is unthinkable for discursive reasoning and not conceivable within dialogue, yet necessary for reason. As such, dialectic utterly dissociates itself from dialogue and becomes the method and driving force that cannot be divorced from philosophy as the enterprise of solitary thinking.

Dialectic as the Art of Thought Exchange. Almost simultaneously with Hegel, Schleiermacher in his *Dialektik* attempts to rethink the role of dialectic in philosophy (or perhaps dialectic attempts to rethink itself through Schleiermacher). He does so by bringing art and thinking together, and by tracing how thinking (*Denken*) becomes knowledge (*Wissen*). Dialectic for him is a "theory of scientific construction" that makes knowledge an "absolute science" or *Wissenschaft*. In such a capacity, dialectic contains the very principles of *the art of philosophizing* (*Philosophieren*), which is not philosophy proper, but rather philosophy in the process of its becoming reflective knowledge, which is the "highest thinking with the highest consciousness."[25] Dialectic thus embraces the very idea of knowledge in the form of a universal. Since, for Schleiermacher, the idea of knowledge is represented primarily in and by mathematics (as it also is for Descartes and Leibniz), there is as much strict knowledge or science (*Wissenschaft*) as there is dialectic and mathematics in any thinking (for Kant, there is as much science in a discipline as there is mathematics).

Dialectic thus represents thinking in its universal aspect—thinking capable of striving toward its highest transcendental ground, which is where opposites as contradictories that appear separate for finite thinking can be reconciled and a unity of opposites becomes possible. Contrary to Hegel and together with Plato, Schleiermacher (who was himself a translator of Plato's dialogues into German and whose work is still widely read) stresses, on the one hand, the affinity of dialectic with thinking that proceeds in terms of opposites without ever overcoming or sublating them. This makes dialectic an *art* (not a science) of "thought exchange" or "exchange of thoughts" (*Kunst des Gedankenwechsels*). Such an art emerges from the "difference of thinking" as the differentiating process within thinking. Dialectic, then, is not an arbitrary process of presenting thought according to the will of the author. Instead, dialectic follows the immanent differences that arise, or rather become evident, within thinking—within an exchange of thoughts—and is itself limited by this differentiation. As such, dialectic is an *organon* of thinking as knowledge (*Wissen*) in that dialectic leads to the "construction of the organism of knowledge" containing all the "formulas" for such a construction. On the other hand, dialectic is also the *art* of a philosophical critique of knowledge, which first appears fragmentary insofar as the fragmentation of thought inevitably emerges in any thought exchange that strives for a conclusion. Dialectic, then, is an artful means (and thus a function or measure of proper knowledge) for situating or orienting any knowledge with respect to its principles.[26]

In his later *Introduction to Dialectic*, Schleiermacher attempts to bring together the ancient art of the "conversational" understanding of dialectic (in Platonic dialogue, which the Romantics hold to be a particularly appropriate artistic form that allows for self-expression and original interpretation) and the modern "scientific" use of dialectic (in Fichte, Schelling, and Hegel, who try to establish philosophy as *the* doctrine of science, *Wissenschaftslehre*, which contains, justifies, and systematically unwraps the very principles of science and strict thinking through dialectic). Schleiermacher distinguishes two types of conversation or dialogue (*Gespräch*). Unlike "proper dialogue" (*das "eigentliche Gespräch"*), which aims at establishing the meaning of a thing and is thus the origin of dialectic, "free dialogue" (*das "freie Gespräch"*) is an act of utter freedom and creativity in which the interlocutors mutually entice each other into a creative "production of thoughts."[27] Dialectic for Schleiermacher, then, is the "doctrine of art" (*Kunstlehre*) for finite thinking. Such an understanding of dialectic stresses its affinity with conversation as an exchange of thoughts capable of presenting the very foundations of the *art of conversation* in the realm of pure thinking.[28] It is noteworthy that for Schleiermacher thinking as artistic must also include the activity of imagination, whereas pure thinking is thinking for its own sake, which simultaneously establishes a measure for both every particular act of thought and the content of thinking.

Dialogical conversation, however, includes not only an exchange between two or more separate and particular thinking beings, but is also reflective, as in Marcus Aurelius. In the latter case such an exchange is a conversation, a dialogue with oneself (*Selbstgespräch*), insofar as one is capable of pursuing two different yet mutually responsive and corresponding trains of thought. Such a split within the thinking and self-conversing subject places the real other within the subject himself, thereby making the subject autonomous and capable of both thinking and knowing solely from within himself. Hence the other is ousted and displaced into the self, which eventually makes the real other, the other of oneself, utterly redundant. Later, Feuerbach argues that real dialectic is not a monologue of solitary speculation, but rather a *dialogue* between the speculative and the empirical that represents both the self and the other.[29] Still, the very existence of the other as the real other is not secure within the dialectical approach and is not secured by it, because the other can, and in fact does, come from the self being split within itself by its own acts of thinking (thinking itself as the other, and the other as itself) and dialectical activity.

Conversation thus has to unwrap itself in the proper way and in an established order that constitutes a method. As the art of the thought exchange, *Kunst des Gedankenwechsels*, dialectic must show, through differentiation and difference in thinking, the principles of knowledge and science that are already implicitly contained within thinking, thereby rendering them explicit in and through conversation or dialogue. Thus far, however, dialectic again appears to be insufficient for clarifying itself by means of itself (even if Schleiermacher's *Dialektik* claims to be an example of dialectic's reflective application of itself), particularly in its relationship to dialogue, from which it originally emerged. It still remains ultimately unclear whether dialectic in its Schleiermacherian version is a *theory* of scientific construction that renders its own grounds explicit by unfolding in the pure and abstract universality of thinking; or whether dialectic is an impersonal (no one's) *art* of thought exchange that stands far removed from any real, personal, spontaneous—and thus not artificial and not artistically constructed—dialogical exchange; or, finally, whether dialectic is but an *organon* that works according to the principles of the art of philosophizing.

Hermeneutical Dialectic. Hermeneutics can be taken as either the art of textual interpretation or the art of understanding the other. Schleiermacher, who establishes hermeneutics as one of the central philosophical disciplines, makes a clear distinction between hermeneutics and dialectic. Hermeneutics for Schleiermacher is the *art of understanding* not only what the other means, but also the art of understanding the other as the other person in speech and text. The task of hermeneutics, then, is to understand the other primarily as an individual in her *expression*, not her content—that is, in her unique "is" and not as a universal "what." Therefore, hermeneutics must be distinguished from dialectic, the *organon* of studying and displaying the "what" and objectified content of the said.[30]

Unlike Schleiermacher, however, Gadamer does not want to separate hermeneutics from dialectic. In its Gadamerian version, hermeneutics is the most recent attempt to reconcile the tradition of dialectic, based on the coincidence of opposites qua contradictories, with Socratic dialogue. Aristotle's logical dialectic already signifies for Gadamer a decay of dialectic, and the logical dialectic of Hegel is utterly monological and oriented toward a single method.[31] But if dialectic can be rethought as "the art of differentiating rightly,"[32] it still has a place within hermeneutical philosophy, which is oriented toward a textual interpretation that would not be altogether arbitrary but might be shared with the other. Gadamer's hermeneutical project is not meant to be a well-defined singular method within a closed system, and it does not intend to confine its interpretive effort of understanding to a particular methodical procedure or set of procedures. Rather, the interpreter has to open himself to the tradition insofar as hermeneutics wants to "stay open" in asking and inquiring ever further. Such an inquiry should bring dialogue back into philosophizing and thus overcome the gap between the dialogical and the dialectical established by the previous method- and system-oriented philosophical tradition.

The art of dialectic for Gadamer, then, is "a perpetual passing from one single thing to another which nonetheless perseveres in the single direction of what is meant and which, for want of cogent deductive proofs, remains in proximity to what is sought *without ever being able to reach it*."[33] Hermeneutical dialectic is thus bound by an immanent logos that embraces the act of speaking and meaning but still surpasses individual opinion, and has such a binding power and such independence from the particularity of the dialectician that even the one who asks and opens up the question remains "in proximity" to the meaning of a text, which is always there yet cannot be grasped by pure logical investigation. In this respect, dialectic is the art of leading a genuine conversation (*ein wirkliches Gespräch zu führen*), and the dialectician, paradigmatically represented by Socrates, is a "not-knower" who paradoxically is aware of his own ignorance.[34] Yet the logos of hermeneutics is always relative to the tradition of textual interpretation.

Hence the very art of questioning *is* dialectic; it is the art of *staying open* for conversation against the established opinions that suppress questioning; it is the art of finding an answer within the horizon of the question. Hermeneutics is thus an ongoing and unending project. The being of hermeneutical dialectic is always in becoming: it is the art of questioning ever further, *die Kunst des Weiterfragens*. The hermeneutic-dialectical enterprise exists in a constant striving to question and interpret a text. And the paradigmatic texts for such an interpretation are Plato's dialogues, which are themselves dramatic, written dialectical (re)constructions of what was said in Socrates' artful oral dialectical questioning.

The primacy of the question and of questioning, which Gadamer finds in Collingwood, means that, in order to properly understand and interpret a text (in particular, a dialogue), one has to understand the question to which the text is an answer. The question, however, is more difficult than the answer, because the question opens up the very possibility of an answer. The question thus must come before the answer, because there can be no answer if the question is never asked. It is the question, and not the answer, that grasps but does not fix opposites in their contrariety and contradiction, which the answer will convey through a "yes" or "no." It is the question's sense that in turn provides direction for the answer.

Unlike sophistic or rhetorical speech, hermeneutic-dialectical dialogue amplifies the other's word, making it stronger, not weaker, because understanding in dialogue is mutual and (if it happens) transforms the interlocutors. Hermeneutical conversation or dialogue should thus be an exercise in dialectic, taken not as a particular (logical) method—as a set of methods or a defined set of procedures—but as an open-ended process of questioning. There is no method for discerning what question should be asked at a particular moment in conversation. The dialectical activity, then, is primarily the activity of establishing the question that will open up a whole horizon within which an answer will be possible.

Dialectic in Gadamer is intended to be a Socratic dialectic devoid of any rigid logical core that would force the interlocutors to move in a prefigured direction and oblige them to provide certain answers. Dialectical hermeneutics must understand the other and the text together with the other within a tradition of interpretation. At the end of hermeneutical questioning, when dialectic, not being the *organon* of thinking (in which respect Gadamer sides with Schleiermacher), coincides with dialogue, there can only arise an understanding of the other or of the text, and yet this understanding is not bound by the discussed subject or an immanent logic of questioning. The hermeneutical movement of asking questions, within which understanding occurs, is everything, whereas the logical end and goal of a dialectically justified conclusion is nothing.

Hermeneutics preserves the incessant striving of live dialogue. Yet hermeneutics cannot preserve dialogue's spontaneity of oral speech, because hermeneutics aims at the interpretation of a fixed written text, even if its interpretation is meant to be open to the understanding of the other. Most important, however, hermeneutics misses the dialogically irreducible other, who is more than just another interpreter. The real other is the one who *is*, the one who not only interprets and understands, but whose being is always involved in a dialogue without its ultimate thematization. Unlike Platonic dialectic, Gadamerian hermeneutics is ultimately about meaning, not being.

Being open to ever further questioning, hermeneutics is not unfinalizable, for unfinalizability presupposes the presence of the personal other who is always explained but is never ultimately explainable. Correspondingly, in hermeneutics it is only the tradition that is beyond individual subjectivity. Hermeneutical dialectic recognizes the other of the text but not the persistent, personal, and independent other of another person or of oneself, who or which would transcend the interpretation of a text within the tradition and be independent of tradition.

Thus one can say that, despite various approaches to understanding the role of dialectic in and for philosophy, modern dialectic still tends to become the *organon* of thinking in the guise of a universal method or general art of thinking, and yet fails to attain such status because it is unable to clearly and unambiguously determine its own position in and for philosophy.

CHAPTER FOUR

Dialogue: A Systematic Outlook

As I have attempted to show so far, dialogical practices give birth to procedures that are first used and then codified, reflected on, and systematized as dialectical methods that are then understood either as a universal method or "tool," like the art of reasoning, or as the most valuable part of philosophy. Dialogue, therefore, is abandoned as philosophically unproductive, unsystematic, and utterly accidental to the process and acts of reasoning. Philosophical thinking thus conceives of itself as having "outgrown" confused and disoriented dialogue and having turned to monological, strict, and conclusion-oriented thinking. However, I now want to return to dialogue once again and, using some of the methods that initially grow out of it, provide a "dialectical" reconstruction of dialogue and examine the features that make dialogue philosophically and ontologically important.

Conversation. Dialectic and dialogue are both related to conversation, and they are connected to each other through conversation. The following four features of conversation appear to respond and correspond to the four main constituents of dialogue discussed below. First, (1) to be in conversation means *to be with the other,* because to converse is to address the other and to be with the other, even if the other is physically absent. One needs the other and thus is never alone in conversation.

Being with the other in conversation means (2) reaching out for the other—*answering* the other and responding to the voice of the other. Answering only makes sense together with asking, because in its very form asking presupposes a reply (or at least the possibility of one), and answering presupposes a question. Each speaker, in turn, becomes a listener in conversation, and vice versa. However, any answer may always yield another question, and any question may multiply the number of possible replies.

The mutual alternation of asking and answering questions implies that (3) the meaning of the subject being debated has not yet been fully extinguished; it needs to be discussed further and is not (yet) accessible to the interlocutors in its entirety. They must proceed step-by-step in order to convey the debated topic. This means that conversation is *discursive*. In this respect, it conforms to thinking, which is "extended" through a number of steps of reasoning and occasionally changes its theme, yet can be always carried on toward the desired (although not always achieved) conclusion. It is not immediately clear, however, if the matter being discussed can be completely expressed by the speakers in conversation.

The very flow of a conversation, with all of its twists and turns, cannot be strictly predicted in advance. Hence (4) there is no method that can instruct the interlocutors which question to ask at a given moment in their discussion, how exactly they should respond, whether they should agree or disagree. In other words, conversation is a *skill* or an *art* that is capable of producing "beautiful" speeches. "Beautiful" here may mean at least two things: either a rhetorically perfected speech whose aim is to persuade by means of its very form; or a dialectically oriented speech, which, even if it does not seem to follow the rules of deduction and reasoning, is not altogether accidental in the direction of its flow and (at least intermediate) conclusions. As an art, conversation differs from the strict method that Descartes and Leibniz had in mind as *the* method of investigation, which would yield an answer to any question posed. Yet it appears that questions and answers are not altogether accidental; instead they are defined by the subject being discussed, by the personalities of those who discuss it, and by the concrete situation in which they find themselves simultaneously together with others.

Furthermore, an answer is always a response to the question that has just been asked, and as such it both continues the flow of the conversation and interrupts it, thereby giving another interlocutor the chance to speak, so that each answer presupposes another question that will follow. However, it is not necessary that in the end the interlocutors should ultimately agree about the topic they discuss and thereby wrap it up into a finalized and logically established conclusion. Here it might be tempting to claim that there is a promise for a certain amount of logic being involved in conversation that can be explicitly formulated. But dialectic and dialogue cope with this promise in different ways: dialectic does so by establishing the formal logical methods (discussed above) for finding out "what" a thing is, and dialogue by always and inevitably implying the components (discussed below) that make conversation a dialogue.

Conversation and Dialogue. I now want to outline a notion of dialogue that further specifies the notion of conversation. It is my claim here that the following four components turn conversation into dialogue: personal other, voice, unfinalizability, and allosensus, all of which answer to and correspondingly complete the four features of conversation mentioned above.[1]

(1) *Personal other.* As I said earlier, conversation cannot occur without reference to the other, to the other person, who is real even if not present (e.g., a dialogue with the dead, which actually became an established genre in late antiquity, most notably in Lucian, and was used in early modernity by French writers). However, dialogue also presupposes an other who is irreducible to either the other person or to the other of the world. This is the *personal other*, the other of oneself. Such an other is often depicted in literature as the subject of address when one talks to oneself as the other, as in Marcus Aurelius' *Ad se ipsum*.[2]

That one addresses oneself as the other does not yet indicate what this personal other is. Dialogue, as a conversation with another person, always involves an expression of one's personal other. The explanation of a point and the discussion of a topic in dialogue always happen with the other and for the other person. Everyone thereby renews the attempt to express herself or himself and speak out as the other.

It is difficult to define what this personal other is, even if it is always present and expressed in dialogue, for the personal other might not be fully and ultimately expressible even if one intends to do so. Indeed, to define something is to put it into final and finalized terms by using logical categories. However, this cannot be done with regard to the personal other because the personal other cannot be expressed in finite terms. The personal other is individual and unique and is always individualized through a person in dialogue. The personal other, however, is also characterized negatively: it is neither the I as the center of reference for all mental content, nor a subject, idea, concept, or function of one's mental or physical constitution. It is not a historical or genetic product, it is not a relation within the dialogical exchange, and it is not a substance. In short, the personal other is not a thing with a clearly and univocally definable essence; but it is not nothing either.

The personal other is a simple whole that is always present and involved in dialogue together with the personal others of all the other speakers. When I talk to others, I am always expressing my personal other and am trying to understand it for myself together with the others. There is, therefore, a plurality of mutually irreducible, and thus independent, personal others involved in dialogue. It seems paradoxical; but every person, although always appearing differently in dialogue and saying different things about different things, is still the same. The personal other is what accounts for the sameness in each person, although it is always expressed in a different manner. Not being a thing—that is, not being a particular this—the personal other is not directly accessible yet it is always expressed through and in dialogue. Since the personal other is not a complete and completed thing with a definite essence that can be described and defined in finite terms, it is not directly accessible and cannot be represented in its entirety. Hence, the personal other is expressed unfinalizably and cannot be exhausted.

But why must we presuppose the personal other at all, which is indeed a strange entity that cannot be properly characterized in familiar philosophical terms? Because being is not an abstract notion, but is rather always a concrete *personal* being in dialogue with the other. In other words, *to be*, and not just to exist, is to be with the other, or *to be in dialogue*, the precondition of which is the personal other that is always fully present in dialogue but is never ultimately expressed in a finalized way.

(2) *Voice.* In dialogical communication, every person is present primarily as a *voice*. Voice represents a minimum of corporeality. Unseen,

the "minimally embodied" voice resides almost on the border between the physical and the mental. Belonging to both, it separates and joins the two. Physical appearance, eye contact, gestures, and touch all belong to personal expressions and play a role in communication. Yet because the voice is what allows a person to converse properly by inviting one into conversation, the voice is inescapable. If a person is veiled in her physical appearance, she can still be dialogically involved with the other as a voice (hence the insuperable appeal of telecommunication). A single voice "alone in the desert" is a *contradictio in adiecto*, a contradiction in terms: a voice must resonate with another voice. Thus the voice is a voice *for* the other and *with* the other. The other who is present as and in the voice, then, is not a bystander, but is rather the other whom one addresses and for whom one tells one's story through rejoinders as well as questions and answers, which can thus be an unfinalizable story.

The voice, then, is in *pluralia tantum*: it can exist only in the plural and yet is a sort of singulative at the same time. It can only be *a* voice together with other voices, one among many that sounds out *now* in a whole plurality of voices. At the same time, each voice is unmistakably distinctive in its individual peculiarities and sonorousness, and is thus uniquely recognizable.

Because each voice is unique it can be considered as what distinguishes a person from the other, and as what presents and expresses a person in her distinctness. At the same time, the voice joins with other voices in dialogical conversation, and therefore the voice connects with the other, including the other of oneself or the personal other, without merging with the other and at the same time without strict separation—that is, without isolation.

Since two voices cannot speak at the same time, each one awaits the other and presupposes its presence in dialogue during the moment of utterance. The other voice is thus present in its anticipation. Therefore the other voice is not simultaneous; yet it is always already meaningfully present in the very possibility of being able to reply to the currently speaking voice. The voice is woven into dialogue through its appeal to the other voice. A person expresses and reveals herself through the voice. Having a voice means having an almost moral obligation to use it in communication with the other. Each voice is capable of addressing the other in a rejoinder, which presupposes and allows for the further continuation of dialogical exchange through questions and answers.

Being unique, each voice is independent. At the same time, being *a* voice with the other it enters into an exchange that can be described as polyphonic. Unlike classical musical polyphony, however, where each voice sounds simultaneously with the others and all of the voices imitate and depend on one another according to the laws of counterpoint, the vocal dialogical polyphony presupposes non-imitative and non-simultaneous interaction, where every voice is independently present yet involved in the whole of the dialogue, which in turn is not dominated by any single voice. Dialogical vocal polyphony, which is still only a metaphor, resembles the linearism of Hindemith more than it does the counterpoint of Monteverdi.

The voice, then, is always *personal*. As such it both expresses a person through her personal other and communicates with the other—it has both an *expressive* and a *communicative* aspect. The voice fully expresses a person through each word, intonation, and utterance—fully, but never finally, because it can always say something new and can always say it differently. But in order to say something by means of a narration that includes, at least implicitly, questions and answers, one can only say one thing at a time and one thing after another. The voice is therefore *discursive*, as is thinking, which has to move from one point to another and tries to present all of the relevant items without omitting anything. On the contrary, unlike the voice, the personal other is expressed only through the voice; it is not discursive. Once thinking decides to "purify" itself—when it decides to move beyond the accidental personal features that are present in dialogue through the voice and on to a systematic investigation of any given topic—discursive thinking then tends to break with dialogue and establish dialectic.

(3) *Unfinalizability*. Another key feature of dialogue is its *unfinalizability*. Even if the personal other accounts for each person's being the same in dialogue, still, no one ever ultimately coincides with herself. Instead, each person is new each time she appears and is therefore other to herself. This makes dialogue engaging and interesting, both to one's interlocutors and to oneself.

That dialogue is unfinalizable means that it is meaningful at every moment and can always be carried on further. Dialogue is an exchange in which the participants can continue to converse with each other without ever exhausting their various relations either with themselves (by expressing their personal other through the voice) or with other persons (by communicating with them through the voice). Unfinalizability also distinguishes dialogue from a mere exchange of information, which is always carried out in a finite number of steps, after which the exchange can only repeat itself.

Unfinalizability, on the one hand, does not mean simply being unfinished or deficient, because a person in dialogue is not a *tabula rasa*, a blank slate on which anything can be written. Rather, she is a unique person in the dialogical unwrapping of her personal other, which she inevitably does anew each time she discusses a particular point in dialogue with the other. On the other hand, unfinalizability does not mean being open to ever further, unrestrained, or endless questioning about a thing or a text either. Indeed, if the personal other is not ultimately expressible or thematizable, then it is neither arbitrarily invented nor accidentally constructed,[3] but rather always there at each moment of dialogical interaction.

Unfinalizability thus means the impossibility of exhausting one's various relations with the other, which include relations with the other of oneself, the personal other. Hence unfinalizability should be distinguished from mere incompleteness. If a person is present in dialogue as the personal other through a voice, then she is not in the process of being accidentally constructed and reconstructed *ex nihilo* according to someone else's intentions or to fortuitous and ever-changing circumstances.

(4) *Allosensus.* Finally, dialogue implies disagreement with the other and the constant questioning of every claim made, which comes from the inability of ultimately and definitely spelling oneself out in dialogical conversation with the other. Such a notion of dialogue goes against the understanding of communication in Habermas, which must (even if it does not always do so) end in a final agreement between the speakers, or a consensus. Consensus terminates the life of dialogue. Moreover, consensus ignores the insurmountable conflict of personal exchange, including political interaction, which is stressed by Hannah Arendt.[4]

A flatly antagonistic conflict is a war that disrupts all possibility of expression and communication in a most violent way. On the contrary, the conflict within dialogue is not a simple dissensus but rather an *allosensus* (from *allos*, "other," as in the inclusive other, or one of a few) or

"*other*sensus." Unlike both consensus and dissensus, allosensus is productive: it allows one to recognize the difference *of* and *from* the other
through a dialogical and unfinalizable unwrapping of the inexhaustible
contents of one's personal other.[5] Using the metaphor of polyphony for
dialogical interaction, one might say that allosensus is present not in an
agreeable musical composition, but in a dissonant yet engaging polyphony
(e.g., in Shostakovich's String Quartet No. 8).[6]

Dialogue. But why are there these four constituents of dialogue (personal other, voice, unfinalizability, and allosensus), and how are they related to each other? One might take the personal other and voice to stand
for the *personal* aspect of dialogue, whereas unfinalizability and allosensus represent its *communicative* aspect. The personal other then might be
considered to present the "what" and voice the "how" of a person's being
in dialogue, whereas unfinalizability presents the "what" and allosensus
the "how" of dialogical communication. In each pair, however, the terms
are neither contraries nor contradictories. Rather, they describe different
aspects of personal being in communication with the other, aspects that
do not exclude but mutually entail each other in dialogue.

Bringing together the four constituents of dialogue, one can say that
dialogue is a process of meaningful yet unfinalizable allosensual exchange
that can always be carried on without repetition of its content and that
implies communication with other persons in the vocal expression of one's
own (but not "owned") personal other.

There may be different classifications of dialogue based on the distinctions between kinds of dialogue, such as the record of a real conversation, the imitation of a discussion, a philosophical dispute over a given
topic, an ideological dialogue (where an interlocutor represents a compre-
hensive view or an established doctrine), or idle chat. Yet any classification
is always only *a* classification, and any system is only *a* system. Here I am
interested in dialogue as a universal form of being as being human—that
is, being in communication with others.

Thus dialogue is primarily *personal*. It is about persons, not about
abstract claims, which can but should not necessarily be discussed or
achieved in a dialogue. Abstract truths are perfectly possible and meaningful, but they belong to their own realm, that of logic, which does
not coincide with that of dialogue. Why? Because, as I argued above,

dialogue involves the expression of one's personal other and communication with another person, who in turn also attempts to unfinalizably disclose her personal other. A dialogue can be a philosophical dialogue in which the interlocutors try to establish a universally acceptable and valid argument, but ultimately dialogue is an ever-renewable attempt to express one's personal other with other interlocutors. It is only through dialogue that a person can be understood by the other, and only through dialogue that a person can understand herself.

Hence dialogue is not about the particular uses of language, and it is not first and foremost a linguistic phenomenon. A dialogue can occur in any language or in many languages at the same time. As a literary form, dialogue was present in ancient epic poetry, was later probably found in the mimes, and was also persistently used and developed in Greek tragedy and comedy as *stichomythia*, or "conversation in alternate lines." Being a conversation, the stichomythic exchange becomes a dialogue proper when the lines disclosing different characters alternate as rejoinders that stand in agreement or disagreement about the point being discussed. Dialogue is thus not constituted as just a conversational exchange of any kind; it is not an accidentally chosen set of sentences set up as rejoinders. Rather, dialogue must unfinalizably reveal a person in a constant non-consensual interaction with other interlocutors.

Dialogue is not about the meaning or lack of meaning of a term that might be formulated in a proposition or a set of propositions. Dialogue is about the encounter with the other as another person. That dialogue is about the person means that no one is (to be) obliterated and no one is (to be) reduced to a common and anonymous denominator. Such an understanding of dialogue is contrary to Charles Taylor's, in which dialogue is an action "effected by an integrated non-individual agent. This means for those involved in it, its identity as this kind of action essentially depends on the sharing of agency (e.g., in threshing). These actions are constituted as such by a shared understanding of those who make up the common agent."[7] Taylor's non-individual, "common" agent is not personal. Rather, *it* is a personification of a community acting in consensual unison according to a certain task. In such discourse, the best one can do is to submit oneself to a smoothly running and established course of common and agreed upon action, which, however, may be doubtful as a joint political enterprise or as an exercise of common will.

On the contrary, there can be no common will in dialogue, and although there is interaction between the speakers, it is *not directed* by an extrapersonal purpose, principle, or agent: each person is free to decide what to do. Not being guided, dialogue results in an inevitable allosensus, which, however, is a kind of disagreement that allows for—and in fact requires—further discussion. Allosensus, then, as a disagreement that allows for the further expression of oneself in communication with the other, cancels out the possibility of a flat consensus. A certain kind of disagreement constitutes the life of dialogue, whereas complete agreement means the death of dialogue and thus also the end of being, if to be is to be in dialogue. In dialogue, relations with the other are not smooth; dialogue implies a disagreement that nevertheless allows for interaction and reciprocal recognition of the other, including one's personal other. This reciprocity between interlocutors allows them to mutually support each other in an ongoing dialogical effort to realize and reciprocally understand the other person and the other of oneself. Not being commonly reduced (and every consensus is reductive with respect to a common impersonal whole), the interlocutors each breathe the same dialogue, yet they do so differently from one another.

Dialogical partners in dialogue are not merged, yet they also cannot be separated. Since dialogue is about human beings and human interaction, it always involves a *plurality* of interlocutors, for a dialogue in the absence of the other is a self-contradictory notion. From what has been said about the personal other, it is evident that dialogue implies *equality* among interlocutors and their voices. Everyone is equal with everyone in dialogue qua dialogical partner. Therefore, a proper dialogical discussion suspends and cancels social and other inequalities.

Since each participant in dialogue is independent and irreducible to any other participant, dialogue is decentered. Any point in a discussion can become its temporary center, and every person is its permanent center, which means that dialogue has many centers at the same time: it is *polycentric*. Dialogue is thus about *freedom* and is the primary locus where personal freedom is exercised insofar as each person, being a partner in dialogue, is never prescribed and continues to contribute to the ongoing and unfinalized effort of dialogue.

Being the locus *of* freedom, dialogue is also the locus *for* freedom. Dialogue has a great liberating potential, which was already known in ancient Greek tragedy and is explicitly mentioned in Euripides.[8] Even though it ultimately does not produce any goods, artifacts, or conclusions, dialogue is a—perhaps *the*—therapy against the misrecognition of one person by another—that is, against the misidentification of a person as having a solely social or other type of role.

Dialogue, then, differs radically from *monologue*. In a sense, monologue is a genuine expression of the Cartesian single-voiced and solitary consciousness that does not need the other or the voice of another, except perhaps for the infinite and unique voice, which the finite monoconsciousness either establishes within itself from the certainty of its own consciousness,[9] or, disappointed and incapable of overcoming its own solitude, altogether rejects. Monologue does not address anyone; it does not expect an answer and thus does not presuppose the other to respond and ask questions, because the monological consciousness itself decides when and which question to ask and what the appropriate answer will be. The other is considered a useful construction in the monological world, which is fully finished, absolutely determined and perfectly petrified in its stillness. Everybody has already and forever spoken. As Bakhtin puts it, the monological world is the world in which people have nothing more to say.[10]

If to be is to be in dialogue, then being qua dialogical is unique and individual, yet it is also plural and shared in communication by and with the other. Therefore there can be no single isolated being, just as there can be no single voice. There is a plurality of being*s* in dialogue who are equal in their capacity to be involved in communication with others by addressing and being addressed. Qua dialogical, being is personal, and qua personal, it is complete and already present yet never finished or finalized: it is always capable of being expressed in a different manner. Qua unfinalizable, dialogue is always renewable and new. Because of this, dialogue is the most engaging and dignified activity proper to humans.

Limitations in Dialogue. The renewability and novelty of dialogue can only be adequately present as and through orality: dialogue is primarily an *oral* enterprise (see Chapter 6). Yet, as an unfinalizable oral exchange, dialogue has its limitations. Primarily, it is limited in the number of its interlocutors. Dialogue already exists between two people, but with each additional speaker the number of possible interpersonal connections increases by many times. There can never be too many interlocutors; however, relations can become too numerous and incapable of being traced in depth, pursued, or sufficiently elaborated in dialogical conversation. Most Platonic dialogues, to the extent that they imitate or reproduce oral dialogue, occur between two or three voices, and some involve four voices. As in a fugue, there are rarely more than four voices being uttered. If there are more than four voices, then each new voice can be heard only when it first appears in the dialogue, after which it becomes woven into the fabric of the discussion. As in a fugue, where only the upper and the lower voices are heard distinctly and the other voices contribute to the richness of the texture, dialogue tends to be confined to two to four speakers (in which case the discussion still usually moves from one pair of interlocutors to another). Because of this, when a Platonic dialogue depicts more than four voices (five in the *Gorgias*, six in the *Republic*, seven in the *Laches*, eight in the *Parmenides* recited by one voice, and eleven in the *Symposium*, which are also impersonated), the extra voices tend to be episodic and sketchy, often only being mentioned rather than speaking for themselves, and do not play a major role in the development of the dialogical exchange. An old prescription suggests that the number of guests at a symposium—the major dialogical event in antiquity—should be no fewer than the number of the Graces and no more than the number of the Muses. This seems to be a reasonable precept.

Dialogue is also limited in its speed, which is defined by the ability of the other to reply and at times retort, and by his ability to understand, to grasp what is said, and to prepare an objection. Dialogue thus has a rhythm of exchange that consists in the movement from one rejoinder to another and causes an incessant interruption by the dialogical partner (see Chapter 5). One can say that, although prosaic in its speech, dialogue is rhythmically poetic. Joining a common rhythm, however, neither obliterates each interlocutor's uniqueness nor makes her part of a common "nonindividual" agent. On the contrary, each interlocutor is what she is only in dialogue and is a dialogical being with other dialogical beings. It is also the rhythm of dialogue that makes it inescapably engaging: with every rejoinder each interlocutor turns toward the other of another person and the other of herself, thereby canceling out the fatigue and constant repetition and boredom of eternal sameness.

Another limitation of dialogue is that it typically consists of relatively short rejoinders. While one speaks, the other is silently present and following what is said while building up to a response and preparing an interruption. In his polemic against the Sophists in the *Gorgias*, Plato argues that brevity of speech is precisely the mark of a speech capable of being properly understood, whereas a long speech only perplexes and bores the interlocutor and prevents him from grasping the point, which in a short rejoinder may not be presented in a rhetorically perfect manner, but is energetically and straightforwardly expressed.[11] Moreover, if one does not grasp the said, then one can always inquire further and ask again for a brief clarification. Herodotus recalls a story about how the Samians once asked the Lacedemonians for help in a long, rhetorically beautiful and elaborate speech, to which the Lacedemonians replied that, having heard the whole, they had forgotten the beginning, and having forgotten the beginning, they did not understand the end.[12] Dialogue is impossible if the interlocutors do not follow and do not understand each other, particularly when their lack of understanding is due to the voluminous nature of the other's rejoinders.

Brevity in speech mirrors the spontaneity of dialogue. Oral dialogue happens in the exchange of rejoinders and cannot wait for its codification or transformation into a properly assembled monological speech or dialogical argument. Dialogue is alive. It is the locus where each participant realizes her being and is intimately present to each of the others without anyone being excluded. In contrast, long rejoinders signify the intention of producing a stylistically perfect and persuasive, and possibly complete, argument. Such an argument, however, ignores the presence of the other, and in fact excludes the other. It does not acknowledge each interlocutor's ability to say what is important in a brief manner—for example, in Wittgenstein's "three words" (as the motto to the *Tractatus* runs)—and it ignores the other's ability to understand what has been said and provide a quick response. Aristotle, who himself wrote a number of dialogues of which we now have only fragments, was probably the first to systemati-

cally employ the technique of alternating brief rejoinders with long disputations. It is probably not by chance that Aristotle advocated a mixture of
imitative dialogue with monologue, for he was the first professional philosophical writer and reader, the first systematic dialectician who wanted
to overcome the inconclusiveness of oral dialogical exchange in favor of a
written and monological, firmly established, and proven logical argument,
the argument that, however, belongs to everyone, and thus to no one.

Dialogue versus Dialectic. In the preceding chapters I have attempted
to narrate episodes in the drama of dialectic breaking away from dialogue,
in which dialectic assumes various masks yet remains the same endeavor
of providing and justifying knowledge and achieving being. In particular,
I have intended to show, by tracing the relationship between dialogue and
dialectic in Plato and Hegel, that while in antiquity dialectic embraces
a number of related but not mutually reducible logical methods that assist in showing what a thing is, in modernity dialectic tends to become
the method of philosophy, and even to be substituted for philosophy by
turning it into a mere methodology. However, both the "ancients" and
the "moderns" agree that the work of dialectic is the work of philosophy.

Despite ongoing discussions about modernity, the very notion of
modernity seems to escape a clear and univocal definition. Being within
modernity, we have to suspend ourselves when reflecting on it. Being
modern, we have to distance ourselves from modernity, particularly by
opposing it to "antiquity," which is to a great extent itself a product of modernity.[13] It appears, however, that one of the focal points of modernity is
the autonomous subject or subjectivity, who or which chooses to think of
itself (him- or herself) as universal. As universal and self-legislating, such
a subject is single and singular, believing that it either already possesses
or generates the whole body of knowledge (or at least the rules and forms
of its production) within itself, and that it extracts such knowledge from
itself by means of special procedures that are understood as belonging to
a strict and universal method. As such, the modern subject poses itself
to itself as not in need of the other with whom one might need to communicate or converse. Therefore the modern subject is monological, as is
dialectic, which is a true expression of the modern subject.

Because of this, as a form of philosophy and philosophizing that at
the outset is one of the major forms that philosophy assumes, dialogue

finds its demise in modernity.[14] To be sure, dialogue was used in a number of key texts from early modernity—in Vincenzo and Galileo Galilei, Leibniz, Berkeley, and Hume. Nevertheless, a modern written philosophical dialogue does not usually occur between concrete independent persons, but rather between interlocutors who represent different abstract philosophical, scientific, and religious positions, among others. In most cases, however, the leading—correct—voice in a dialogue turns out to be the variously disguised voice of the author himself.

Unlike dialectic, dialogue discloses the personal other of each interlocutor through interaction with the dialogical other. The dialogical other is always being expressed but is never ultimately thematized; it cannot be other than it is, yet is always present and presented differently. However, dialectic lacks any presence of the personal other, as well as other constituents that characterize dialogue. Dialectic does not need the specifically human component, does not presuppose the uniqueness of a person or a personal other, whereas dialogue is impossible without it. In fact, any particular "this" is an obstacle for dialectical argument and reasoning, because dialectic needs to speak about the universal, about the essence in and of each particular thing and not about its individual differences. As Leibniz puts it, *individuum est ineffabile*. Indeed, a unique thing has something that distinguishes it from every other thing and is not covered or explained by a general form or essence. Hence a "this" is not grasped by a universal theory or method, especially if "this" is a personal one capable of spontaneous, free, and unpredictable behavior. Any given theory can only declare individual traits to be accidents, and thereby safely remove them from the list of subjects it considers. Only dialogue allows one to utter one's unique—and mysterious—individuality, not through theoretically verified definitions, but rather as something that can be expressed as the same, yet each time anew, in communication with the other. The participants in dialogue always share an unrepeatable dialogical situation with unique persons as interlocutors.

The objective of dialectic, on the contrary, is systematic knowledge, which is arrived at through the efforts of ordered discursive reasoning that in turn must ultimately be enfolded within and overseen by non-discursive thinking. The objective of dialogue, on the contrary, is communication and expression, which presupposes discursivity and cannot be overcome in the inalienable presence of the other. Here dialogue is understood as oral dialogue because, as I said earlier, Platonic written dialogue is an artful imitation of live dialogue and is therefore concerned with dialectical reasoning, which in turn does not require a personal other that it would have to portray in its uniqueness and recognizability. Dialectic is thus *impersonal*: an argument can be anyone's argument. Dialectic is everyone's, and thus no one's. Somebody has to be the first to discover an argument, but anybody can repeat, reproduce, and use it. If dialetic requires certain skills of argumentation in order to decide where to go at each step, then dialectic is personal only in the sense that each dialectician, as a skillful practitioner of investigation and questioning about the nature of things, has her own personal *style* of inquiry. The result of reasoning, however, should always be the same—a universal abstract truth.

Therefore, the person in dialogue is not established theoretically through a logical argument, but instead is revealed through narration, even if at times it may be redundant or repetitive, or even a matter of simply fooling around. In other words, dialogue must have a *narrative* component, which is absent from dialectic. Narration is what allows dialogue to be dramatic and to express the process of either discussing a point or disclosing the personal other. Unlike dialogue, dialectic does not require narration; it does not recognize or need the ironic yet sincere Socratic pretense of not knowing or ignorance: dialectic wants to lead to knowledge. Discursive thinking is not narrative: it tells a story about correct reasoning, but the plot in such a story is an ordered argument and the only character that coincides with the author is discursive reason itself. Unlike dialogical narration, the dialectical story, once it is proven correct, cannot ever be otherwise, although it is possible that there is a different way of expressing the truth about something—that is, a different proof of a universal statement. Therefore, the dialectical order of an argument is not that of narration. Dialectic follows its subject through a strict and immanent logic of reasoning that occurs in a finite number of steps and is not concerned with the story of the personal other that can always be continued and told differently by a different narrator. Because of this, there is a certain boredom in dialectic, which, once it has established something, can only repeat itself, whereas dialogue is an activity that is always appealing; one never tires of joining in.

No wonder, then, that dialectic does not recognize a personal *voice*. As such, dialectic is *monological*: any dialectical argument or particular method can be invented, used, and appropriated by anybody and in solitude. Hermeneutics recognizes the individual voice of the interpreter, but such a voice is neither personal nor dialogical in the sense being described. Both dialectic and dialogue have a claim and interest in understanding what cannot be otherwise. Dialectic realizes this interest in an abstract, finite, final, and definite argument, whereas dialogue realizes it in the concrete universality of a complete yet inexhaustible person. In its universality, dialectic is mute, whereas dialogue is vocal. Dialogue can be dialectical, but dialectic is always monological and hence not dialogical.

Modern reason is preoccupied with its own self-transparency and self-accessibility, particularly with establishing the transparency (through a precise order of steps, each of which clearly follows from the premises and previous steps) of the proofs it produces and spins out of itself. In a sense, dialectic is an expression of this anxiety. Dialectic is a way—often taken to be *the* way—to the truth of things. Dialectic has to be able to trace and fix each stage of reasoning and engrave it forever into a reproducible, universal, and anonymous (impersonal), argument. However, any of these ways is only *a* way insofar as it can be undergone differently to the desired end. Yet the end of dialectical investigation—namely, establishing the essence of each thing in and by the argumentative disputation of reason with itself—must be achieved at the end of the argument in a finite number of steps and in accordance with certain formal logical rules, which justify the conclusion that has been arrived at and makes it forever definite and true. Dialogue, on the contrary, is never finalized insofar as it can never be completed in a finite number of steps but can always be carried on meaningfully and without a repetition of its contents. Because of this, dialogue always seems uncertain. Yet it is only as *unfinalizable* that dialogue can be the locus for the certitude of the meaningful and always inextinguishable expression of a human being in communication with the other.

Finally, the mode of non-consensual interaction, a particular kind of disagreement that I have called "allosensus," which is productive and capable of recognizing the difference of and with the other in dialogical interaction, is completely lacking in dialectic. Any disagreement in dialectic must ultimately be resolved and brought to a standstill in a well-established conclusion. This conclusion can occur either through the sublation of contradictory opposites (which, although they struggle against each other, are nevertheless united and reconciled within a closed and finalized system) in speculative, systematic dialectic, or through a productive disagreement of non-understanding (Schleiermacher's *Mißverstand*, as different from a mere lack of understanding, *Unverständnis*) that is suspended by understanding in the interpretative hermeneutical dialectic. Or disagreement may be overcome in logical, formal dialectic by means of an argument that is meant to be universal and binding, such that everybody (every "rational being") must agree with and accept the force of the deduction obtained.

Thus one can say that dialogue differs from dialectic in that dialogue clarifies and allows for *being* as pluralistic and as a live being with the other, whereas dialectic studies and orders the *meaning* of a particular thing or term, including the meaning of being as an abstract notion. Hence dialogue belongs to both anthropology and ontology, whereas dialectic belongs to logic. Dialogue and dialectic, therefore, have different spheres and rules of functioning, which some thinkers (most notably, Hegel) try to unduly match and identify.

Dialectic, Dialogue, and Art. Finally, I want to return to the question of the relation of art to dialectic and dialogue. Nowadays, no one knows what art is; or rather, one is left with the chance—and even the need—to elaborate one's own understanding of art. However, in antiquity and recently in modernity, art is taken to be an imitation of nature. As such, art must produce close (often embellished) imitations of what is independent of, and exists apart from, the effort of art. Yet today it is not clear what nature is because, on the one hand, people appropriate and domesticate nature by reconstructing and fitting it to human needs and thereby create artificial, unnatural surroundings. On the other hand, in early modernity nature is studied by exact science. But in order to become the subject matter of precise mathematical description, matter has to be taken as an abstract lifeless uniform extension, as a construction of the inquisitive scientific mind. Because of this, nature as spontaneous, living, growing, self-reproducing, and self-organizing is lost in and to contemporary thinking. It is not by chance, then, that there is no philosophy of nature in contemporary philosophy, but rather only philosophies of specialized scientific disciplines, none of which asks about nature as such. And because there is no longer any nature to imitate, the traditional conception of art as the imitation of nature does not make sense anymore.

Owing to dialogue's spontaneity and unfinalizability, there can be no definitive systematic theory of dialogue, although of course dialogue can be the subject of philosophical consideration, which makes it possible to discern and discuss the constituents of dialogue. If dialogue does not allow for a theory, then it does not allow for a science either. Is it, then, an art? To be sure, dialogue requires certain conversational skills, perhaps even a gift or talent, in order not only to speak to the other and to express her personal other, but also to listen to the other. Still, unlike dialectic, which may produce remarkable proofs and refutations that are worth preserving in writing for future generations, dialogue *does not produce anything* and so is *not* an art. The reason for this is that dialogue is not about production (in this respect, it is not "poetic") but about communication (with the other person) and expression (the expression of one's personal other). A dialogue may end in an argument that creates a logically justified conclusion or shared understanding, but it does so only accidentally. Because dialogue is renewable—meaningful and yet unpredictable at any given moment—any conclusion that may be achieved is always only *a* conclusion. In this sense, dialogue does not conform to the traditional division (which itself might be one result of a dialectical reflection on dialectic) between science, art, and method.

Dialogue also has features that it shares with art: dialogue can be imitative, although only as a carefully reproduced and written (e.g., Platonic) dialogue, whereas oral dialogue does not imitate anything. Written dialogue may be imitative as, on the one hand, a dialogue that portrays characters in their coexistence and responsiveness to one another (a literary and dramatic dialogue), and, on the other hand, as a dialogue that depicts the development of arguments (a dialectical dialogue). Oral dialogue, which is being with the other in conversation, is therefore a phenomenon of life, spontaneous and live. Oral dialogue is thus neither an art nor a method.

Dialectic, on the contrary, is a planned and premeditated enterprise. Already in Plato, dialectic has features of both science and art, but it cannot decide for itself which one it is. Why? Because even if dialectic is capable of arriving at a sought-after conclusion (although this is not always the case in Plato's Socratic dialectical dialogues), it can never be sure that it will do so, that a formulated claim will indeed be established by an argument. There is no way to tell or decide what question to ask and in what direction to move at each point in reasoning and argumentation. Rather, such decisions are a matter of skill, and hence of art. Or they are a matter of genuine ingenuity, which is a gift or "genius" in the Socratic sense, a non-reflective capacity that guides the reasoning that one may use without knowing what it is. Dialectic, then, appears to be a logical art, an art of reasoning, of asking and answering the right questions. However, dialectic is a conversation that is restricted to asking about and possibly finding "what" a thing is. In this respect, dialectic is much more narrow than dialogue.

At the same time, dialectical reasoning is capable of proving a point and demonstrating what a thing is in a strict and logically justified way. As such, dialectic bears features of science or strict scientific method. Throughout the history of philosophy, dialectic appears to be somewhat arrogant in its attitude toward dialogue. Dialectic tends to consider itself a "higher" and stricter discipline than dialogue because dialectic strives to avoid all of the accidental features of individuality and context and to distill its arguments into pure theory based on universal statements. The very ideal of strict science, or *Wissenschaft*, comes from the standards of dialectic.

One of the major problems for philosophy, from antiquity through contemporary thought, is the role and place of logic in philosophy: is logic *a* method, *the* method, an *organon* or instrument of thinking, or first philosophy itself, the very core of philosophy devoid of its anxiety about being? Does logic prescribe the rules for (correct) thinking—or does it describe the rules of acting through thinking and language that appear only when acting? Similar problems arise with dialectic in its relation to philosophy due to dialectic's initial proximity to logic. One could say that these problems are still unresolved, or at least that they have been resolved very differently by different philosophers.

Emerging from a seemingly unruly and spontaneous dialogical conversation with a real other, dialectic tries to express and spell itself out as a way of grasping and systematically presenting the regularities within thought, which, even if they are not always definitely expressed, always shimmer behind the dialogical exchange. Dialogue is unfinalizable, always different, live, and spontaneous, and hence not a systematic enterprise. In this respect, dialogue differs from dialectic, which wants to structure itself as, and is historically understood in terms of, a logical *system*.

Because dialectic initially structures itself as systematic, it aspires to be the strictest and most precise among the available means of reasoning: the rational, logical science of being. The *precision* of dialectic is that of an exact reference and a firmly and clearly established order of steps in reasoning. But oral dialogue has its own measure of precision, which in a way even surpasses that of dialectic. Seemingly imprecise yet much more flexible, oral dialogue is capable of conversational finesse, of rendering a discussion ever more precise and attuned by means of asking the appropriate questions when and as needed. Indeed, in an oral exchange one can always ask for further concise clarification, and then ask again if something remains unclear. An example of such an exchange from a literary work is the conversation between Natasha and Pierre in *War and Peace*: the more detailed the distinctions they try to make in their conversation, the worse they understand each other.

Living and alive, dialogue is also *self-organized*. Its self-organization comes from its being personal: dialogue is personally organized—that is, it is organized by each person who is involved in, expresses, and unwraps herself in and through dialogue. Moreover, everyone performs such expression while communicating with others in a commonly established and shared rhythm of allosensual exchange. Dialectical reasoning, on the contrary, is organized by something external to it, namely, by the task of providing a rationally justified conclusion about a thing and by the skill of the dialectician who uses dialectical tools and devices in searching for such a conclusion.

Dialogue may be about theory, but it is not primarily theoretical. Dialectic, in contrast, has universal aspirations. There can be a dialectical account of dialectic's structure and functioning. In other words, dialectic is inclined toward theoretical *self-reflection*: there are numerous dialectical discussions of dialectic, whereas dialogues about dialogue are rare. There are, however, dialogical reflections about dialectic (e.g., in Plato), but there is almost no dialectical account of dialogue because of dialectic's condescending attitude toward dialogue as not being properly theoretical (which is obvious in Hegel).

Although dialectic must classify everything according to a definitive measure and ultimate order, dialectic itself appears to escape any definite classification. Dialectic tends to overcome the limitations of finite thinking and the accidents of oral dialogical exchange—of time, place, personal character, sudden interruptions and changes of topic—by elevating itself to a necessary discipline of reasoning. Still, as I have argued, dialectic cannot eventually decide whether it is an art, method, or science. The reason for this indecision is that the logos of dialectic, the set of rules and procedures it uses to clarify the meaning of a thing, is immanent to dialectic and can thus be made explicit only through its self-reflection. Such self-reflection, however, is rarely successful, because the task of dialectic, as the "eye" of discursive reasoning, is to see and clarify "what" a thing is, and not to clarify seeing itself.

Therefore, dialectic in its solitary and monological self-reflection seems unable to determine what it itself is. From the very beginning, when it makes its first appearance in the Socratic logos and Sophistic disputations, dialectic undergoes a sort of permanent identity crisis insofar as it cannot decide what it is as such or what it is in and for philosophy. Put in traditional terms, dialectic is neither an art nor a science, neither a theory nor *the* method, neither a logical "instrument," or *organon*, nor the most valuable part of philosophy, and yet it possesses certain features of each.

Once again, the history of the relationship between dialogue and dialectic appears to be the following: genetically, Socratic conversation gives birth to oral dialogue, which is live and spontaneous. On the one hand, oral dialogue makes written dialogue possible as a literary and philosophical genre. And on the other hand, oral dialogue brings about dialectic, which originally appears in conversation and then is established as formal thinking and the logical organization of thought. Emerging from dialogue (Plato's written dialogues are already deliberately constructed as dialectical), dialectic eventually becomes the manifestation of an impersonal, solitary, self-isolating, thinking subject that spins out a web of logical categories from within itself. The dialectical subject does not need a personal other who is persistently present in dialogue and withstands any attempts at being constructed, invented, or used by the subject. The single dialectical subject acts not in the spontaneity of dialogical exchange, but instead lives off the pure logic of abstractions. Modernity begins with (and perhaps forever terminates in) the monological and dialectical subject, who (or rather which) exiles and substitutes the dialogical person by making her the object both for and of abstract dialectical thought.

Thus dialogue differs from dialectic in important ways. Dialectic and dialogue are not reducible and should not be reduced to one another. Each one works well within its own sphere and is suitable for those who are engaged in it for different purposes: in dialogue, for communicating with others and for the expression of one's personal other, and in dialectic, for attempting to find out what a particular thing is.

CHAPTER FIVE

Dialogue: Interruption

Dialogue as a Series of Mutual Interruptions. The modern universal and rational subject appears both dialectical and monological. Yet, having been repressed, dialogue always returns in unexpected ways in philosophy, literature, and especially human interaction. The constancy and robustness of dialogue may mean that it is indispensable for personal communication and therefore paramount for personal being—that is, for being a person. Or, contemporary interest in dialogue may go hand in hand with the criticisms of modernity and modern constructivist subjectivity. Even if there is no "scientific" discipline of dialogue that is similar to a monoconscious and monological science of knowledge, still dialogue—both spoken about and used—may be characteristic of contemporary thought. One might say, perhaps, that opposing monologue to dialogue as though they were mutually exclusive is itself a product of the reflective self-criticism of "moderns" in the first quarter of the twentieth century, when the most significant discussions of dialogue occur, not, however, within a single systematic discipline, but in a set of observations and closely related practices.

As I have argued up to this point, dialectic is a logical cognitive enterprise. As such, it presupposes an unbroken chain of steps in an argument and series of arguments, and therefore an uninterrupted movement of monological thought. Now I want to show that there is another critical distinction between dialectic and dialogue: that dialogue is essentially based on *interruption*, which is lacking in dialectic. I will do so by providing a close reading and interpretation of a short text, followed by a discussion of the work of interruption literature in philosophy (Plato) and drama (Beckett).

An important contribution to modernistic discussions of dialogue in the 1920s belongs to the school of Formalism in linguistics. Of exceptional interest is a brief yet groundbreaking article by Lev Yakubinsky, "On Dialogic Speech."[1] Yakubinsky begins by making a number of observations on communication, which he understands as always implying a debate, the paradigm of which is a scholarly oral presentation followed by a discussion. His major claim is that oral communication does not consist in a series of premeditated and calculated monologues, nor in a well-conceived, orchestrated, and directed dialogue, but rather in *interrupted dialogues.* As such, live oral dialogue is based on the constant *interruption* of what is being said. Therefore, dialogue consists in a series of mutual interruptions that are spontaneous yet still respond to the previous rejoinder in the context of the whole discussion.

One should emphasize that the interest in dialogue for Yakubinsky is primarily linguistic: he is mostly concerned with the investigation of communicative structures of speech and language. As I have argued in more detail elsewhere, however, dialogue is not solely a linguistic phenomenon, but is also the very human condition in and through which people are persons in their communication and co-being.[2] Besides, contra Yakubinsky's strategy of beginning with "empirical observations," I should say that, while the concept of interruption can be *described* with reference to empirical observations, it nevertheless *cannot be justified* by reference to any one of them: the justification of interruption can only come from a philosophical analysis.

Yakubinsky's main thesis is that communication presupposes dialogue, which in turn presupposes a progression of constant mutual interruptions. But dialogue is not just an exchange of questions and answers, because, as I have argued, such an exchange can be arranged as a preordered dialectical proof that reveals its conclusion through the motion of deduction according to certain logical rules—a movement of reasoning in which each answer is already implicitly contained within the question and thus does not allow for a spontaneous answer, an unpredictable reaction, or an interruption. If dialogue is "characterized by the alternation of rejoinders" (p. 250), then a rejoinder (an utterance) always comes as a response to another rejoinder, which provokes still another rejoinder, etc. . . . Because dialogue is unfinalizable, there is no limit to the continuation of such an exchange within dialogue itself or even in the topic being discussed (which can always be considered from another perspective or simply changed), except for human limitations, such as the number of interlocutors, the number of possible objections that we can attentively uphold at one time, our becoming tired relatively quickly, and so on. There may be a certain order in oral dialogical exchange, but this is not the same as the rigid order of dialectical discussion, which is imposed on a discussion by the very logic of argumentation. Rather, dialogical order is that of mutual interruptions: interruptions "dictate the course" (p. 250).

As I have argued, dialogue presupposes a mutually shared action of dialogical partners, to which, however, they remain irreducible. The mutuality of dialogue means that each interruption is both invited and anticipated by the previous rejoinder. As such, dialogue is constituted by the interruptible speech of the other, rather than by an impersonally arranged order of speaking. Mutuality also presupposes the interaction of a plurality of participants: actors, speakers, and listeners. But if there are many independent actors present in dialogue, then there is no preferred or single center of panoptical subjectivity; there is no single focus of dialogue.

Because of this, "any interaction between persons," as Yakubinsky puts it, "is inter-action. By definition, it strives to avoid one-sidedness; it tends to be mutual, dialogic, and therefore eschews monologue." Monologue, then, "is a highly artificial form of language . . . [that] reveals its true essence in dialogue" (p. 249). As such, again, dialogue differs from a preconceived and artificially constructed monologue, which, historically and genetically, has emerged from dialogue as an artful and post-dialogical construction. Monologue is one-sided, which means that it serves one or a few purposes such as evaluation, feeling, rhetorical persuasion, stressing a particular attitude, establishing oneself in a position of superiority over the other, and so on. To be successful, correct, or beautiful, monologue therefore must serve a pre-established purpose. In other words, monologue is preconceived and carefully calculated. Hence, whether oral or written, monologue is artificial and is intended to displace dialogue. As such, monologue can be meaningful only under deliberately established, special (artificial) anti-dialogical conditions, which include following a respectable *ritual* or ceremony both strictly and precisely. The monological ritual is then secured by acknowledging an accepted *authority* that must protect monologue from undesirable incursions and interruptions. (An example of such a ritual is scholarly talk or presentation, which is introduced and directed by a moderator whose task is to prevent unsolicited interruptions and to orchestrate, after the monologue of the speaker, an orderly discussion, which in turn often only consists of a series of monologues.) As I argued above, monologue suits a single, autonomous, and calculating subjectivity and is irritated by any unruly plurality of speakers or unordered utterances.

Monologue, however, cannot contain or prevent dialogue. Monologue only *provokes* dialogue, even if such provocation occurs internally, for dialogue accompanies every monologue and always wants to interrupt it, to break its usurped and solipsistic speech. Moreover, a listener cannot abstain from reacting to the uninterrupted flow of either oral or written monological speech by means of facial grimaces, gesticulation, notes, underlining, or any other form of expression—whether mental, oral, or written—that the listener can manage (p. 250). Sometimes interruption, as a provocative disruption of a monotonous or outright corrupt action, takes the form of Cynic diatribe (ancient, in Diogenes; modern, in Rorty) that is uttered publicly and intended to cause a scandal, which should necessitate the continuation of dialogue.[3]

The very meaning of "interruption" points in this direction (even if etymology does not prove anything): *interruptio* in Latin can mean a "break," "gap," "pause" or "division." Interruption, then, is a break of the monoconscious monologue, of its well-conceived and yet stiffening plan. Interruption is a gap within an otherwise evenly running argument that suddenly takes unexpected turns. Interruption is a pause taken by the speaker in order to allow the other to act and react against the original and provocative action, thought, or utterance. Interruption is a division of speech into distinct yet interconnected, mutually responsive, and responsible rejoinders where each voice remains unique yet is still heard throughout the dialogue. An interrupted dialogue thus disturbs the consensual smoothness of a monolithic and monological speech, whether it is a dialectical argument or a rhetorical attempt at persuasion. Monologue only remains uninterrupted insofar as the subject isolates itself from the other and shuns the other's unexpected—live—interventions.

Furthermore, the prefix *inter-* can have three different meanings in Latin: "between," "from time to time," and "perishing." All three of these meanings seem to be present in interaction and interruption: both presuppose an action (whether it is a theoretical discussion, a shared moral deliberation, or just idle chat) that occurs *between* the speakers, where nobody can usurp the privileged position of making an ultimate judgment. Both interaction and interruption occur suddenly in response to the other's word, and no one can plan or assign in advance the proper time (*kairos*) for such interaction and interruption. Only dialogical partners can themselves decide, judging from the appropriateness of the situation and context of what is being said, when is the right time for interaction and interruption. Finally, both interaction and interruption point at a certain uneasiness in dialogue. Dialogue is not a smooth conversation that results from a shared consensus or agreement. Dialogue is more of an exchange of rejoinders that, on the one hand, presupposes a lack of ultimate transparency and understanding of the other and his word, and, on the other hand, allows for the continuation of a debate in which the non-erasable difference of and with the other is recognized through a form of disagreement, which I have called "allosensus."

Interruption brings interlocutors together into dialogical interaction not as incommensurable and isolated individuals but as dialogical partners, without, however, blurring their personal distinctions. The "rupture" concealed in interruption is not the one that separates, but rather the one that unites interlocutors as partners in a shared, single dialogue. The breach in conversation provided by interruption allows one to break through to the other, including the other of oneself, and approach being-together in dialogue with the other. Interruption therefore allows one to gain an adequate, though perhaps forever incomplete, glimpse into the other's word. The mutuality of interruption, therefore, always accompanies dialogical interaction with the other, which opens up (although never completely) a "window" to the other, and hence to co-being in dialogue as being with the other.

Dialogue should be taken as an interaction that presupposes—

allows and indeed requires—the possibility of being interrupted. Dialogue is interruptible, and thus renewable, at every moment. Yet oral dialogue is spontaneous, which means that there is no rule indicating when to interrupt or what to say exactly. Only the interlocutors themselves can decide when to exchange the roles of the speaker and the listener, or of the questioner and the answerer. When interrupted, the participants still "intend to complete their unfinished utterances after the interlocutors' rejoinders" (p. 250). Any interruption presupposes the resumption of the interrupted rejoinder. When being interrupted, however, an interlocutor still intends to continue spelling out what she was saying in the rejoinder right before she was interrupted. But she must also respond to the intervention, and thus interruption will inevitably change the course of one's intended speech. In other words, interruption always brings an unexpected and inevitable novelty into dialogue, such that a preconceived rejoinder is always corrected by an interruptive (counter-)rejoinder.

In dialogue, every rejoinder is meaningful *per se*, even if and when the speaker is utterly perplexed—for example, when during his rejoinder the speaker is still trying to understand, formulate, and express a response to what the other has just been saying. Of course, the other may be just as perplexed, and even when he is not trying to say, understand, or express anything meaningful, his speaking is still a reaction to what was previously said, so that what might not have made sense before suddenly becomes meaningful.

Moreover, any rejoinder makes sense within the larger "whole" of dialogue, which is perceived as such by the interlocutors yet is never fully accessed by anyone at any particular moment because the dialogue is unfinalizable and can always be continued further. The "whole" of dialogue is not given in advance and is not preconceived or calculated, both because it involves unique personal voices and because it presupposes constant interruptions that cannot be predicted or planned. Thus every rejoinder is recognized as a distinctive "unit" in dialogical exchange, yet it forms not only part of one's enunciation but also part of the "whole" dialogue.

My rejoinder is meaningful both in itself and as a response to the other's interrupting rejoinder, which, although it has not yet happened, nevertheless must be anticipated. The interrupting "unit" of a rejoinder and the "whole" of an interruptible dialogue mutually presuppose each other. The peculiarity of the situation consists in the fact that even if a rejoinder "awaits" interruption it is still unknown when the interruption will occur and what exactly its response will be. However, the "whole" can never be given, completed, or fully thematized, and therefore my rejoinder is meaningful in the anticipated yet never given "whole" of a meaningful and unfinalizable dialogue. At the same time, a dialogue is itself meaningful only due to the possibility of constant mutual interruptions of its interlocutors' rejoinders.

Every rejoinder is released, then, with the implicit understanding that it will and should be interrupted, because only then can a rejoinder be meaningful. But if an interruption has not yet occurred, and since each rejoinder will be interrupted in its turn, no rejoinder can be fully anticipated in its ultimate formulation and meaning. In Yakubinsky's aphoristic formulation, "we may describe the alternation of utterances in dialogue in the following terms: while one interlocutor 'is not done yet,' the other 'is already continuing'" (p. 250).

Interruption therefore has two aspects: it is the act of changing and exchanging rejoinders; and it is the act of intervening with a concrete rejoinder that responds to the previous one(s) in the context of the unfinalizable whole of a dialogue. Every interruption, then, is the concrete realization of a course followed in dialogue: an interruption is a particular choice made from a range of possible responses that are allowed at this moment both by the previous rejoinder and by the "whole" of the dialogue.

In other words, each utterance qua interruptive is independent, yet it also responds to and is responsible for another interruptive utterance. The almost spatial "whole" of dialogue does not fit within linear discursive speech and reasoning, but instead always shows itself as meaningful (and in this sense complete) yet oscillating between the mutual responses of a dialogue that is "not yet done" but is "already continuing."

The Work of Interruption. What, however, is interruption? In dialogical interaction, interruption is the insertion of a rejoinder by an interlocutor while the other interlocutor's utterance is not yet dialectically complete but is already dialogically complete. "Dialectical completeness" means the logical completeness and unity of an argument in its entirety and ordered steps of reasoning from premises to conclusion. "Dialogical completeness," in contrast, refers to the "whole" of a dialogue, which is present at each moment and in each utterance of a dialogue but is never fully expressed or finalized.

Interruption is mostly exemplified linguistically, through speech and language, which includes gestures, facial expressions, etc. Contra Yakubinsky, however, I want to argue that interruption is not only a linguistic phenomenon. As the very condition for the possibility of dialogue, interruption is a breaking through to the other person within dialogue, whereby one's interaction with others is never finalized or dialectically complete but is still meaningful at each moment.

Hence nothing can really be said or thought without interruption, even if it is an interruption of oneself in an inner dialogue with oneself as the other.

Once again, dialogue is a series of mutual interruptions. Yet from our childhood we are taught that interrupting is *impolite*: to interrupt is to fail to take seriously the autonomy of a self-legislating will that is assigned to oneself and the other, who is an independent and isolated subject of moral and theoretical deliberation. This is of course a serious reproach, yet it might be answered that even if not interrupting someone is meant as a sincere sign of attention, of attending to the other in her entirety and worth, nevertheless, non-interruption is self-subversive and performatively self-contradictory. Indeed, to let the other speak without interruption is to recognize her action as a complete and completed monologue, and thus as isolated and cut off from any possible dialogical interaction. In dialogical interaction, each actor is a partner and as such is unique and independent but at the same time is freely included in the dialogue. Obviously, dialogue cannot exist without participants, and yet each interlocutor is not reduced to being a mere part or constituent of dialogue. Being independent, each one still responds to the other's rejoinders and anticipates them in her own interruptible and interrupted speech.

Put otherwise, there are no individuals who are monological subjects in dialogue. The indivisible and isolated autonomous subject is impersonal and implants itself anonymously into each person. In dialogue, dialogical participants are independent, and each one contributes to the never fully preplanned or pre-determined whole of a dialogue. Thus, to be interrupted does not mean being "shut up," which is the monological murder of the other. Interruption means the continuation of dialogue with attention to–attending to—the other. To be uninterrupted is to be isolated, whereas being interrupted is to be included, invited, and recognized within dialogue, which now becomes the forum for common action and inter-action. Because of this, only in dialogue can a person realize herself fully—but never completely—as a person, as a dialogical partner in a constantly renewable, interruptible but never fully finalizable dialogue with others.

In this sense, *not interrupting* is impolite, because if I do not interrupt the other it means either that I am not interested in him and what he is saying, or that I do not know what to say, or again that I am just waiting for my turn while the other finishes his monologue, so that I may utter mine.

The ideal of non-interruption in the guise of politeness fits the interest of the monological, solitary, and isolated subject. Through non-interruption, the monological subject tries to maintain the illusion of total self-reliance, autonomy, and independence—primarily independence from others. Such a subject wants to think of itself (not him- or herself, since it is impersonal) solely from within, as necessary and unique, as indivisible and individual, exemplifying the "light of reason," which shines forth from within itself. Because of this, the modern subject does not need, and does not tolerate, interruption. Intolerance of others is put in the form of unconditional rules, particularly that of non-interruption, whose power is disguised as respect for others. But in fact it is respect for oneself as the autonomous subject who is satisfied with letting others be respected. (In fact, the categorical imperative is likewise a demand for non-interruption.)

No wonder, then, that non-interruption also becomes the ideal of modern dialectic, which is meant to be the method utilized by the universal rational subject for extracting all possible truths in an orderly manner, doing so solely from within the subject itself in a continuous, systematic, and uninterrupted flow of thought. To interrupt such evenly progressing monological thought is to commit a crime against truth and prevent its being extracted within monological thinking and speech. The modern subject, however, is abstract because it is everyone and no one. The lonely subject isolates itself from other equally monadic subjects of unconnected—no one's—monologues.

Interruption, then, does not break the continuity of communication and personal expression with others. Constantly interrupted and interruptible, dialogue is still continuous by being constantly performed through the common effort of the participants, where each one retains her unique personality and independence.

In other words, interruption is incompatible with the ideal of the individual as an indivisible and self-sufficient subject. Because interruption presupposes that dialogue is decentered around a plurality of independent actors, interruption is offensive and in a sense deadly for the singular and abstract subject. Dialogue may thus be considered as knowing—in the sense of a skill or an art, rather than a method or a discipline—*how* and *when* to interrupt. One might even say that a culture can be defined in part by a dialogically accepted and acceptable way (or ways) of interrupting the other.

That dialogue consists of alternating rejoinders follows from the possibility of constant interruption. Without interruption there is no dialogue. Hence, if we are in dialogue then we are interrupted, we should be interrupted, and we should interrupt. This means that when we are in dialogue we are aware of the possibility of interruption and we anticipate it. "Our participation in dialogue," says Yakubinsky, "is determined by our expectation of being interrupted, by our awareness that an interlocutor is preparing to respond, by our fear that we might not be able to say all that we want to say" (p. 250).

The other's rejoinder, as such, might not explicitly insist on a response, yet it still invites an answer. On the one hand, each rejoinder is meaningful by itself even if it is perplexed or confused. On the other hand, every rejoinder is meaningful in the context of the "whole" of a dialogue in which every interlocutor participates and always shares. Therefore, being in dialogue presupposes (1) awareness of the possibility of interruption; (2) anticipation of the "when" and "what" of such interruption; and (3) a certain lack of certainty (a "fear") that one might not be able to fully anticipate the other's rejoinder, because the way a rejoinder actually occurs is often unexpected, even for the author of the rejoinder.

According to Yakubinsky, responsiveness in dialogue, which is grounded in the dialogue's interruptibility, presupposes a *duality* of tasks, namely "the reception and understanding of another's speech and preparation of our response" (p. 251). I would think, however, that the situation is even more complex than simply implying the duality of understanding the other and providing a response. Preparing a response is in many ways similar to evaluating a combination in chess, choosing one among many possible moves and strategies, and thinking through the best option as far as possible. Indeed, interruption may be undertaken for the sake of clarifying the other's speech; or it may also be a response to the other in a spontaneous reaction to what the other says. A response implies a multiplicity of tasks that need to be formulated *simultaneously* while listening to the other. These include: understanding the other, preparing a satisfactory response by choosing the best one among a number of possible and meaningful replies (e.g., raising an objection or providing an elaboration); anticipating the other's response to one's own response and then offering a satisfactory response to the other's response to one's own response; etc. One must inevitably stop because one cannot go on into infinity and one's ability to calculate (especially quickly) is limited. Unlike in chess, however, dialogical interaction is fast; and most important, there is often no clear indication when a dialogical partner has actually made her move or when it is now one's own turn to move in response.

Thus each dialogical partner is in a situation of constantly having to make decisions based on his understanding of the other, preparing a response that will make sense both as a response to the now continuing—and not yet finished—concrete utterance, as well as with respect to the context of the whole dialogue, which, however, may change with each rejoinder. Each reply, meaningful and complete as it may be, could also have been otherwise because it is just one (possibly the most appropriate) realization of many possible replies within the whole dialogue, which in principle can always be continued further.

Dialogical partners may or may not know each other. In the former case, each of them knows the other's style of discussion, and thus they are better able to anticipate the other's answers and even the very moment of interruption. If the interlocutors are not familiar with one another, they may request clarification of what is being said as well as its context, and then prepare a response. Interruption for the purpose of clarification may also arise while attending a speech that is prepared in advance.[4]

The situation gets even more complex, however, because each listener in dialogue has to decide when it is appropriate to interrupt the speaker.

Since, however, there is usually more than one listener, each one must also decide *who* is going to interrupt at this moment, prepare a response while another listener interrupts, and consider how to adjust her response with respect to each new interruption.

Moreover, the complexity of one's tasks in dialogue is bounded by one's limitations and inability to perform each task promptly and in full, particularly in comparison with the situation where one has a chance to prepare and think about a response without time constraints and without the pressure of responding to the other's rejoinder.

The constant presence of interruption in dialogue, in both its possibility and its necessity, has important consequences for dialogue, insofar as being in dialogue presupposes knowledge of *how* and *when* to interrupt. A number of dialogue's features are implicit, then, in its interruptibility.

Dialogue is constituted by an exchange of rejoinders: when one interlocutor is speaking, the other prepares a response while waiting for the right moment to interrupt, after which she, in turn, will be interrupted. (Occasionally more than one participant will talk at the same time, which can sometimes render dialogue incomprehensible but at other times can create a perfect fugue.) Dialogue thus presupposes (i) a *rhythm* of interruption that is established when a dialogue's participants all join the exchange in which each rejoinder is meaningful by itself yet is always made in the context of the whole dialogue. In this sense (but only in this sense) dialogue as interruptible presupposes Taylor's "sharing of agency" (but not an "integrated non-individual agent"). As in ballroom dancing—or in syrtaki group dancing—dialogical partners have to follow a commonly established and supported rhythm. This common rhythm presupposes the already mentioned *mutuality* of interaction and interruption. In dialogue, however, the shared rhythm differs from that of dancing, because in dialogue the rhythm is not imposed on the participants by music, which comes "from without," but is kept by a common dialogical effort and activity, which comes "from within."

Furthermore, because dialogue is a rhythmically organized exchange in which rhythm is established by alternating interruptions, dialogue presupposes (ii) a certain *speed*. In particular, dialogue is characterized by *brief* rejoinders. Each rejoinder should be relatively brief because once it begins turning into a long monological speech it will inevitably be interrupted by the other; otherwise the dialogue will lose its rhythm and momentum and will simply stop. Because of this, the exchange in dialogue is quick.

In ancient considerations of dialogue, particularly in Plato, brevity (*brakhylogia*) was already characteristic of dialogical speech, as opposed to sophistic speech, which is prepared in advance and is both monological and lengthy.[5] Such lengthiness produces the effect of boredom. As Yakubinsky notes, if, for some reason, the interlocutor speaks slowly, then "we are irritated and disturbed and consider delay inappropriate" (p. 251). Dialogue, on the contrary, which consists of short, interchanging, and energetic rejoinders, is engaging because everyone is involved in the interaction through participation and interruption.

Since dialogue consists of relatively brief rejoinders, it combines the spontaneity of dialogical interaction with the quickness of deliberation and response. As I argued before, only oral dialogue is "immediate" and spontaneous, whereas written dialogue can always be prepared in advance: even its spontaneity and interruptions can be carefully calculated as imitations of oral dialogue. In this respect, written dialogue is much closer to monologue than it is to oral dialogue. Moreover, written dialogue lacks such communicative means as gesticulation, facial expressions, intonation, and the like (p. 251). To be sure, in oral dialogue one's self qua personal other is also mediated by one's voice, but written dialogue greatly increases such mediation.

Because dialogue is quick and consists of relatively short rejoinders and at the same time moves within the aforementioned "not yet done," "already continuing" structure, no point in a dialogue or any part of it can be considered complete. Yet any point in dialogue, as well as any of its parts, is meaningful to the interlocutors and those who attend it—those who remain in dialogue with the others. Dialogue thus can always be carried on without any repetition of its contents. In other words, dialogue is complete in its incompleteness. (As such, dialogue is similar to a living being, which or who exists as the same being yet is always different, and as different is always the same.)

Put otherwise, dialogue is always (iii) *partial* yet "dialogically complete." Seemingly unguided, dialogue is nevertheless well organized, both by its topic (although a topic can always change during a discussion) and by its participants (each one's self as one's "personal other" is constantly expressible yet never exhausted in dialogue). Thus interruption reveals a most important feature of dialogue, its being unfinalizable.

The brevity of dialogical speech, its incomplete completeness, and the complexity of dialogical tasks all make dialogical rejoinders (iv) *simple*. Because we are under constant pressure in dialogue owing to the possibility and necessity of interrupting and being interrupted, we have to pay more attention to "what" is said and "what" we ourselves should say than to "how" to say it. Language provides us with the "how," whereas we, as dialogical beings, are responsible for the "what."

Simplicity in dialogue means that dialogical speech is *stylistically imperfect* and somewhat rough. At the same time, dialogue is *compositionally simpler* than a monologue or a monological dialectical argument constructed to be a dialogical exchange. However, both dialogue and monologue share the same syntactic structures, which monologue, as a product of dialogue's disintegration, borrows from dialogue's simple yet not simplistic speech.

Although dialogue is not necessarily an exchange of questions and answers, as is required of dialectic and is explicit in any dialectical argument, dialogue often invokes such an exchange. An answer given in oral dialogue usually requires fewer words than one given in a written and stylistically perfected monological imitation of oral dialogue. The reply in a live dialogue is often a simple "yes" or a "no" or an incomplete sentence: it is *short*. Such a response is brief because it is understandable from and within the context of what is said, and because a long, stylistically correct, and "sophistically" seasoned answer irritates others.[6] The reason for this is that an elaborate and long rejoinder causes delay and makes one's dialogical partners wait and suspend their answers, which are constantly being prepared, changed, and held in an effort to accommodate the complex task. This task presupposes (1) listening; (2) understanding; (3) preparing a response; (4) choosing the right response and the opportune moment of interruption; and (5) overcoming the fear of not being able to say what one intends and wants to say, especially when one is not ultimately sure what one really should or can say until the very moment of actual speech.

Often, we simply do not have time to prepare an answer as elaborate as a complete sentence (even if we are taught to speak in full sentences, in dialogue we tend not to use them); nor are others willing to endure a long rejoinder. Understandability and the steady rhythm of a quick dialogical exchange are ultimately preferable to the rhetorical niceties of monologue. Rhetoric persuades, but dialogue allows one to live and be.

Interruption in Philosophical Dialogue. In order to further illustrate how interruption works, I now want to consider the structures and strategies of interruption in written—philosophical and literary—dialogue. I begin with Plato, not the inventor of philosophical dialogue yet probably the best dialogue writer of his time, when literature was not yet considered as separate from philosophy.

Except for the *Seventh Letter*, all of Plato's works are, or contain, dialogues and therefore utilize interruption, which is indispensable for the constitution of dialogue. The Greek verb for "interrupt" is *hypolambanein*, which literally means "to take up by getting under," but in discourse also means "to take up what is said," "to retort," or "to rejoin" with a sense of disbelief or objection, and "to interpret or understand in a certain way," in particular to purposefully misunderstand and thereby take the other unawares.[7] Plato uses this verb and its derivative participles several times in the *Republic* in order to introduce a new speaker who then intervenes in the dialogue. Thus Polemarchus interrupts Socrates and Cephalus (331D); Glaucon interrupts Adeimantus and Socrates (372C); and Adeimantus interrupts Socrates and Glaucon (419A). At *Republic* 338D Thrasymachus complains that Socrates distorts or misinterprets his words, which of course Socrates does purposefully and ironically in order to interrupt the (incorrect) development of Thrasymachus' speech (cf. *Euthydemus* 295C, where the irritated Euthydemus accuses Socrates of the same). In the *Euthydemus*, one of his most subtle dialectical and eristic dialogues, Plato portrays two Sophists, the brothers Euthydemus and Dionysodorus, who come to Athens in order to teach wisdom to young people by instructing them in the art of argumentation. The two teachers of wisdom, however, do not intend to teach about how to arrive at "what" and "how" things are through their discussion in speech. Rather, following the Protagorean program (frag. B6b DK) of making a weak argument, logos, the strongest one, they promise to teach young men the art of winning any debate or oral contest. Their suggested method is to refute *any* proposition the interlocutor might advance in response to a proposed question.

Since any proposition can be refuted by the proper means and by applying learned argumentative skills (at least this is the claim), *both* a thesis and its opposite or antithesis can be refuted. Moreover, not only are both of the opposing claims refutable, but they can both be considered true at the same time.[8] This means for the Sophists that the very question of true statements existing independent of techniques of argumentation and refutation is meaningless. What matters is the ability to win a contest by *any* and all available means—to struggle not so much with a question or thesis, but with the other interlocutor. Sophistic dispute is an agonistic enterprise for the sake of victory: it is a war where anything goes and any means will suffice. Winning a dispute over a question, then, is a personal achievement of an eristic pugilist against the other (not by chance, the two brothers began their careers in Athens as wrestling teachers, *Euthydemus* 271C–D), and does not even presuppose searching for an impersonal and universal truth about a certain matter, the gaining of which would be everyone's victory.

In the Platonic dialogues, except for the seemingly simplistic yet very complex and subtly nuanced figure of Socrates, the interlocutors mostly appear to be somewhat schematic, because the argument they are about to utter is more important for Plato than are the characters' personal features. The two brothers in the *Euthydemus* are portrayed as boastful and overconfident, yet with voices that can hardly be distinguished. Their prey, the young Clinias, whom they choose to exploit in order to demonstrate their own argumentative skills, is a somewhat naïve and straightforward interlocutor. However, Clinias is capable of recognizing, with some astonishment, his failure to answer the original question, in which sense he is closer to Socrates, who often must also recognize with irony and surprise that, despite all his efforts to find the right answer to a question about what something is, he cannot arrive at a satisfactory conclusion. At the same time, Socrates is also close to the Sophists in being exceptionally skilled at questioning the other. Socrates, however, differs from the Sophists in that, first, he is able to see the cause of an apparent contradiction and disclose it, and second, he recognizes the meaningfulness of looking for an interpersonally valid answer, which might not actually be found, but that in its very possibility renders the dialogue both ongoing and meaningful.

It is important to note that the *Euthydemus* is a dialogue that is retold by Socrates, and that when Socrates "retells" the speeches of the two brothers to Crito (most likely, Plato invented both speeches and the very occasion of their retelling), Crito *does not interrupt*, but listens attentively. All of the internal interruptions in the speeches therefore belong to Socrates, who, in order to be able to reproduce them, must *interrupt himself* by imitating interruption, which in this case *is* interruption.

In order to persuade the Athenian youth, Euthydemus and Dionysodorus stage a play of questioning they have rehearsed in advance, in which they each refute an opposite thesis through prearranged mutual and multiple interruptions. In this way, they seem to prove that no answer and no proposition is possible, and thus that any answer is possible.

With a fiendish pleasure, and even before Clinias has a chance to answer his question, Dionysodorus tells Socrates that, however Clinias responds, he will be refuted anyway. The Sophistic practice of interruption in dialogue is thus not only elenchic but also eristic, insofar as it is capable of disproving any claim not by means of dialectic (at least, not only), but rather by any available disputational means or tricks.

At 275C sqq., Euthydemus asks Clinias: Who learns, the wise or the ignorant? Clinias' answer is that the wise learn, which is immediately refuted by Euthydemus: since the wise already know, they are not in need of learning. So, he says, Clinias is wrong. Dionysodorus immediately interrupts by pointing out that the wise are more capable of learning and memorizing what is taught, and therefore that it is the wise, and not the ignorant, who learn. So Clinias is right. Therefore, Clinias' claim is both right and wrong. A little later, after a series of similar perplexing interrogations by the two brothers in which each assumes an opposing and contradictory position, Socrates comes to Clinias' rescue (277D–278E): the problem might be resolved by pointing out the ambiguous and plurivocal application of each term, which is used differently in each of the seemingly opposed positions. The solution to the problem lies in referring to Prodicus' program of "distinguishing names." In the first case, "wise" means "already knowing," and in the second, "wise" means "capable of learning."

Dionysodorus' interruption occurs immediately after Euthydemus' dubious intervention. Taking up the argument as if catching a ball (277B),

Dionysodorus throws it back to Clinias just to show that this time the opposite answer is not viable. Hence, once again, anything—and nothing—can be proven, and therefore anything goes. Sophistic interruption, then, is a premeditated interference, an intrusion whose sole purpose is to disallow the interlocutor from thinking for himself about the matter being discussed and prevent him from revealing the intentional fallacy.

Socratic dialogical dialectic is thus based on interruption that uses appropriate and unambiguous questions and strives toward correct and straightforward answers, most of which are already implied by the questions. Dialectical interruption intends to connect the interlocutors' reasoning about the matter in question with "what" that thing is, and not, as in sophistic interruption, to persuade by any means. Sophistic interruption, on the contrary, only imitates the argument and spontaneity of interruption in live dialogue.

As Socrates ironically notes, the wisdom that the Sophists promise to teach is a *sophia amêkhanos* (275C), a wisdom that is both inept and awkward, as well as extraordinary and irresistible. Such wisdom embraces opposites rhetorically, not dialectically, and if there is a process of passing from one contradictory opposite to the other, it is done by means of eristic devices—through the interruption of the other by a prearranged interference on the part of the other sophist whose intention is to interrupt the interlocutor by stunning and shutting her up (or down).

Sophistic learnable knowledge is thus opposed to Socratic learned ignorance. Sophistic "wisdom," which the Sophists are eager to teach, is the wisdom of the eristic elenchus whose interruption stuns thought and breaks up live discussion. Socrates' dialogical elenchus is powered by the love for wisdom, which he claims not to have and thus cannot teach. His questioning only aspires toward wisdom as knowledge, which seems possible yet is never fully achieved in Plato's dialogues. The Sophists are rich in money and wisdom. Socrates is lacking in both. Both the Sophists and Socrates use dialectic and interruption in dialogue, but they do so differently. The Sophists interrupt the other in order to gain an advantage over him, whereas Socrates interrupts in order to extract from the other what he always already has but does not yet realize. It is through dialogue that the Sophists show themselves wanting and indeed poor in wisdom, whereas Socrates is rich in wisdom without, however, possessing anything for himself.

Interruption in Literary Dialogue. Since without interruption dialogue cannot be meaningful or even exist, interruption plays a central role in drama. For drama *is* written dialogue that is either read or performed in a theatrical play, as well as in a radio broadcast play, in which characters are purely dialogical voices and are heard but not seen. Beckett explores and uses a whole spectrum of interruptive devices in *Waiting for Godot*, which in a sense is based entirely on interruptions.[9] First, the characters *always* interrupt each other, at times very abruptly. Sometimes their interruptions take the conversation in a new direction that is loosely or seemingly not at all connected with the previous one, and sometimes by interrupting one another the speakers support each other's unfinished rejoinders, thereby completing them, only to be interrupted again.

Interruption, then, is the very nature of the characters' *interaction*: they interact through and by interrupting each other, which at times creates the effect of a sudden loss of meaning and orientation with the chance of regaining it only later. (All meaning will eventually only be gathered after Godot arrives, which remains the subject of the characters' waiting, hope, and faith.)

In most cases, interruptions are *fortuitous*. As such, they do not follow any "logic" or "inner consistency" of a character qua voice, but are used by the author to structure and construct the plot. It is unclear, however—and such lack of clarity itself becomes the text-structuring principle—whether the author already has a plot and "main idea" in mind, or whether the plot is instead constructed while the play is being unwrapped, written/performed/attended, and listened to, or whether there is no plot at all, and whatever one takes to be the plot is completely accidental and arises as an arbitrary interpretation of mutually and self-interrupting rejoinders within parts and pieces that are randomly brought together.

In some instances, the characters (Vladimir and Estragon) interrupt each other by complementing and bringing each other to completion through perplexity, disputation, stubbornness, and being tragic and comic at the same time.

> VLADIMIR: Charming evening we're having.
> ESTRAGON: Unforgettable.
> VLADIMIR: And it's not over.
> ESTRAGON: Apparently not.
> VLADIMIR: It's only beginning.

ESTRAGON: It's awful.
VLADIMIR: Worse than the pantomime.
ESTRAGON: The circus.
VLADIMIR: The music-hall.
ESTRAGON: The circus. (p. 23; cf. p. 40)

In addition, *self-interruption*, when a character interrupts himself, plays an important role in marking his interaction with the other. Often, self-interruption is an attempt at self-understanding (again, with the other). Self-interruption also signifies an effort to remember something (pp. 40, 42), to recollect an absent(-minded) meaning. Such a rejoinder consists entirely of mutually interrupting parts. And at times, remembrance is attempted by interrupting the other (p. 39).

Interruption is often also accompanied by mutually addressed interruptive gestures and actions. Self-interruption, too, occurs through gestures and motion: Vladimir "remains a moment silent and motionless, then begins to move feverishly about the stage" (p. 37).

Beckett is clearly aware of the importance of interruption, to which, in fact, there are explicit references: Pozzo is angry at being constantly interrupted, but as he calms down he finds out with a bit of frustration, disappointment, and self-irony that he is unable to gather any meaning from what he was saying and thus cannot but keep interrupting himself.

POZZO: (angrily) Don't interrupt me! (Pause. Calmer.) If we all speak at once we'll never get anywhere. (Pause.) What was I saying? (Pause. Louder.) What was I saying? (p. 20).

When Vladimir and Pozzo think they have spotted somebody and then quickly realize their mistake (nobody is there), they each simultaneously begin renouncing the other's mistake, which thus turns out to be the recognition of each other's error (pp. 47–48). They begin the same phrase simultaneously, simultaneously interrupt each other (and thus themselves), then ask pardon for their interruptions. "Vladimir: I interrupted you. / Estragon: On the contrary." Then, they recognize their own (and thus each other's) mistake, and immediately become angry and curse each other.

Beckett uses pure interruption to create suspense and produce gaps between rejoinders that open up the possibility for multiple interpretations of what is said when all of the potential meanings and psychological nuances are hinted at but never fully exhausted.

(Silence.)
POZZO: And thank you.
VLADIMIR: Thank *you*.
POZZO: Not at all.
ESTRAGON: Yes yes.
POZZO: No no.
VLADIMIR: Yes yes.
ESTRAGON: No no.
(Silence.) (p. 31)

Since the characters are interwoven and very close (Vladimir and Estragon have known each other for "fifty years maybe" [p. 35]), such pure interruption is on the one hand almost self-interruption, and on the other hand it is the completion of what is said as a whole, wherein one of the voices might assume the role of the other (in the above example, Estragon's "No no" rejoinder instead of Pozzo's anticipated "No no" response).

Interruption may also express utter bewilderment on the part of a character while he tries to gather himself, as when Estragon simply repeats what Vladimir says (pp. 38–39), which is meant to help Estragon overcome his frustration and be happy.

The silent character, *kōphon prosōpon*, has an important role in the play in that he does not interrupt anybody, yet thereby provokes others to interrupt each other and themselves. Insolently addressing the speechless Lucky in a master/slave manner *à la* Hegel, the speaker, Pozzo, wants to regain his own proper speech, but can't: getting no answer, his rejoinders remain brief, rude, and disruptive exclamations. The silent character retorts and interrupts only by violently kicking Estragon. A verbal interruption happens only once, when Lucky breaks his otherwise non-responsive monological silence and is *ordered* to think—which itself is a contradiction, since thinking is a free act promoted by a common dialogical effort. Lucky then produces a long and meaningless pseudo-philosophical and pseudo-theological monologue, which is *the only* uninterrupted speech in the whole play (pp. 28–29). Yet even this long speech constantly interrupts itself; but the interruptions do not make it any more meaningful. However, when Vladimir tries to imitate such monological and uninterrupted "thinking," he simply *cannot do it* (p. 47), for his own thinking is partial and incomplete. He rarely comes to any conclusion, but at least his thinking occurs together with that of the other, Estragon, and is thus real even though it is confused, since it is properly interruptive, interrupted, and dialogical.

Finally, the rejoinders in mutually interruptive speeches are *brief*— quick and short—and as such constitute the *brakhylogia* in much the same way that Socrates characterizes it in the *Gorgias*. Undeniably, Beckett also uses some of the Sophists' techniques, even if he is not aware of doing so. Thus Vladimir and Estragon appear childish, but when they meet the messenger boy (the "angel") for the first time, they turn into impatient and rather ruthless interrogators. They begin questioning the boy while constantly interrupting each other, so that the boy does not know whom to answer. Both times that Vladimir questions the boy (or boys, if they are indeed different on different days), the exchanges parody Socratic dialectical dialogue, in which each answer is already implied by the question itself. The "dialogue" between Vladimir and the boy(s) is quite similar to the "dialogue" between Euthydemus and Clinias, in which the perplexed and intimidated boys (the messenger and Clinias, respectively) answer either "yes" (more often) or "no" (pp. 32–34, 58–59). The interrogation, however, does not produce a definitive answer: Godot has not (yet) arrived, and Socrates and the Sophists have not (yet) found (although for different reasons) a solution to the problem concerning the correct definition of a thing.

Conclusion. Interruption thus should be understood as an interruption of the other's speech that is indispensable for dialogue insofar as it allows multiple, independent voices to continue the work of spelling themselves out in the rhythm of simple, quick, and partial exchanges with the other in a constantly renewable attempt at breaking through to the other. A lack of interruption characterizes lengthy and systematic monologue (for instance, the present uninterrupted discussion of interruption). Furthermore, one can distinguish different kinds of interruption.

(A) Interruption of the other person, of the *interlocutor*, can be done for the sake of either (1) interruption, or (2) the continuation of a *thought* as it is expressed and developed in dialogue. This kind of interruption is represented in the written medium of a literary or philosophical dialogue, and as such is *imitative* of oral dialogical interruption.

When an interruption of the other is meant to interrupt a thought, it can be either (1.1) a Sophistic interference, which may represent one's apparent and simultaneous support of both a thesis and an antithesis, or a seeming disproof by reducing *any* given thesis to a contradiction, including its antithesis, by *any* available means, such as an argument's being fallacious and logically illicit. This can be done either (1.1.1) for the sake of *persuasion*—to gain the upper hand in, for example, a (political, legal, or everyday) dispute and establish one's opinion as the accepted one; or it can be (1.1.2) practiced as *play* (a "game of learning" [*tōn mathēmatōn paidia*] [*Euthydemus* 278B]) for the sake of amusement or simply to perplex the other who is unable to follow the game and join in.

Besides, (1.2) the interruption of an individual or commonly shared thought (including self-interruption) may contribute, mostly in literature, to the development of the plot, in which case it is carefully calculated by the author. This sort of premeditated interruption may derive both from the character and from the author, even if the author might not have a definitive plot in mind, in which case the plot is in a state of constant construction and reconstruction. The author may also introduce a new speaker who intrudes on the conversation. Alternatively, the task of a staged or inadvertent intervention may be entrusted to an interlocutor who is already involved in the conversation.

Finally, (1.3) the interruption of a thought may intentionally or unintentionally be rendered paradoxical and aporetic (as in Aristotle's *Metaphysics* B or *Physics* Z). An aporia is precisely that moment of dialectical "non-viability" (which is the literal meaning of "aporia") or interruption that points not so much at a mistake in one's deduction, but rather is a productive tip for the further development of a thought, or even points at the need for a radical change in the whole theoretical framework.

However, the continuation of a thought that follows from the mutual interruption of characters may also be considered (2.1) Sophistic, if it is done for the sake of extending a speech and eventually bringing it to a conclusion that will be accepted by all the speakers, even if that conclusion is fallacious and the means of persuasion are doubtful.

Furthermore, (2.2) the continuation of a thought through interruption (that of the other interlocutor and of oneself) may be a device (again, used mostly in literature) either (2.2.1) for the continuation and unwrapping of the plot, in which case it essentially performs the same task as (1.2), or (2.2.2) for each character's use in expressing something that is each character's own—an isolated thought or something inscribed in the uniqueness of each character that is independent of and even contrary to the author's intentions and the immanent logic of the plot's development.

Finally, (2.3) the uninterrupted maintenance of a thought may be dialectical for the sake of an argument. In this case, an argument is considered justified if its conclusion can be—and actually is—arrived at in an uninterrupted sequence of steps that proceed from accepted premises by means of shared rules of deduction, whereby the conclusion is either already known or is reached at the end of such reasoning. This uninterrupted motion of a thought is dictated by the thought itself, by the problem in question, and by the structure of questioning. Thought has to move in a certain correct ("dialectical") fashion, where no two steps of reasoning are confounded, and where the end or conclusion can be reached and kept in sight. The justification of a thought in and by an uninterrupted dialectical motion is therefore indispensable to the self-completion of that thought. Its motion might even transform itself into a unique system (as in Hegel's *Logic*), in which seemingly separate and singular statements become a single, monoconscious, and monological whole, where they appear necessary for its completion and thus overcome the multitude of interlocutors and banish dialogue as accidental.

Contrary to this, (B) mutual spoken or oral interruption on the part of interlocutors is spontaneous. Being dialogical, interruption does not need to follow an established pattern of dialectical exchange. Mutual interruption is live and personal. It implies both the interruption of a thought and its continuation at the same time. A thought in dialogue is interrupted insofar as each interlocutor, supported by the other, may continue developing a particular thought or the speakers may move on to discuss another one. Still, a thought in dialogue also remains uninterrupted insofar as it can be preserved and considered from different perspectives, and even sometimes abandoned and lost, then found again and kept alive in ongoing conversation. Only this kind of interaction may be considered properly uninterruptible, because it is practiced for the sake of the unfinalizable realization of oneself with the other. Such spelling-out and expression, both of oneself as one's never fully exhaustible and personal other, and of the other person, occurs together with the other only in spoken dialogue.

CHAPTER SIX

Against Writing

Dialectic and Dialogue, Written and Oral. Dialectic thus arises within live and interruptible dialogue as a reflection on the methods and procedures of questioning that might lead to the correct conclusion and definition of what a thing is. Unlike dialogue, however, dialectical speech tends to be long-winded and detailed because it has to follow a precise order in an uninterrupted series of steps in reasoning. Once considered worth preserving, dialectical speech and its imitation in artificial philosophical dialogue are better off seen as an itinerary for thought, a sort of ancient *periplous* (sailing map) or subway map, because in this way they can be easier preserved, transmitted, discussed, developed, and manipulated.

As I have argued, oral spontaneous dialogue is a particular kind of conversation: marked by the presence of the personal other and a plurality of voices, dialogue is unfinalizable and allosensual. Moreover, dialogue is oral, and as such it is often unguided and at times even chaotic. This kind of dialogical exchange does not need to be recorded or written—it only needs to be continued. And it is systematically distilled into the *art of dialectic*, which tends to rid itself of the possibilities and accidental limitations of live dialogue. By transforming dialogue into a way of presenting arguments and not persons, dialectic conceals oral dialogue and makes it unrecognizable.

If dialectic comes as a product of disintegration of oral dialogue in the form of written *elenchic* disputative dialogue, then I have to disagree with Havelock, who takes the development of logic—and hence dialectic—to be possible only because of the introduction of alphabetic writing in Greece.[1] His argument appears to imply circularity: if he is right, then dialectic as an ordered written enterprise is founded in oral dialectical disputation, which itself must be rooted in writing, and hence writing is based on writing.

Dialectic has its place in literature, in rhetorical disputations for instance, and in poetry, where dialectic is particularly present in the epigram, which moves in terms of opposites either satirically or in a desperation that reflects the suffering of the "split soul," *mens diducta* (as in *amo et odi* in Catullus' famous *amo et odi* [Catullus, *Carmina* 85]). Mostly, however, dialectic is established as a logical and method-oriented way of constructing valid proofs in accordance with the rules that are already implicitly present in oral discussion. Dialectical reasoning presupposes the development of a sound argument, the proof of which may require a (very) long, although finite and complete, sequence of steps in a strict and correct order that is defined by the formal rules of deduction. This succession of dialectical steps itself follows the logic of thinking and reproduces its discursivity. Once established, however, the sequencing needs to be maintained. Hence dialectic is essentially a *written* enterprise because writing is more effective than human memory at storing lengthy lists and the exact details and particular path of an argument through which discursive thinking had to proceed in order to establish a proof. To be preserved, an argument (a philosophical, logical, or mathematical one, e.g., in Plato's *Parmenides*, Aristotle's *Analytics*, or Euclid's *Elements*) needs to be written. A proof must be reproducible. But once it is forgotten, not all of its minute features can be repeated. When it can no longer be considered a sound proof, it again becomes a hypothesis until it is recollected or proven once more and perhaps in a different manner.

At the same time, oral dialogue is at the origin of the *art of dialogue*, which is dramatic, literary, and written. Writing is artificial. Written dialogue as a genre is artificial because literature is artificial, and in this respect it is an art; only oral dialogue is "natural" (even though it is not a part of nature). Literary dialogue is a skillful imitation and reproduction of live dialogue—not a copy, but rather a sophisticated redressing of oral speech intended to present characters within the development of a plot in a literary work. Literary dialogue is already distinct in epic poetry and is further perfected by the Greek tragic poets, by Platonic philosophical dialogue, and by satirical Menippean dialogue. Later, however, in the philosophy and science of the Renaissance and early modernity, literary dialogue degenerates into pedagogical and catechismal dialogues that present and defend a single "correct" view belonging to the author or to a whole school of thought.

Written, Spoken, and Heard: The Oracular. The consideration of thought as represented in the forms of being both spoken and seen occupies a major place in Plato's work. In one of Plato's most celebrated and commented upon passages at the end of the *Phaedrus*, Socrates and Phaedrus discuss the appropriateness of putting speeches in writing (*graphē*)—that is, of drawing a portrait of fluent and momentarily existing words by a sequence of signs.[2] Plato entrusts to Socrates a rather precarious situation of discussing oral speech by means of oral speech itself, which occurs in a well-constructed written graphical dialogue that at the same time paradoxically intends to undermine itself by arguing that a written text is secondary to oral speech. The situation is even more ambiguous because Socrates does not write but only—always—speaks. As a result, Socrates refuses to appropriate a speech (*logos*) about the relation (also *logos*) between the oral and the written, between what is spoken and what is etched into text. Instead, he (re)produces a speech that seemingly retells the argument and entrusts it to the oral tradition that transmits the "heard" (*akoē*) through myth and rumor.

Oral speech is spoken and heard. In retelling the other's logos, Socrates chooses, as he often does, to impersonate the other's voice, usually doing so with a bit of irony. Socrates is a great actor who withdraws his own personality in order to let the other (another person, or even "the laws") live through him.[3] This time, Socrates allows two different voices to speak through him. In so doing, he must liberate his speech—if not altogether from his own presence, then at least from any interference on his own part. By speaking in different voices, Socrates speaks neither from nor for himself. In order to become capable of allowing others to speak through him, Socrates must become empty and free himself from himself in a *sui generis* purification, a cathartic expulsion ("vomiting") of his own self that would provide a place for others to speak in and through their voices freely and without distortion.

The modern monological thinking subject is monoconscious and thus exclusive of the other. Hence the monological subject is incapable of opening itself toward the oracle and of being taken seriously as the voice of the other. By contrast, Socrates assimilates himself with a *pythia*. The *pythia*, the Delphic oracular priestess, is the one who rejects herself, her sane mind, in order to allow the oracle to pass through her freely and become manifest through uttered words. In this way, Socrates impersonates what is right and true (*alēthes*), ascribed to the interest-free and therefore supposedly non-distorting oral tradition of what is "heard."

In dialogical conversation with Phaedrus, Socrates substitutes one of his own rejoinders with a dialogue within dialogue that he retells in its entirety. This allows him to liberate himself from himself and thereby transmit only what is "heard." Of course, Socrates makes up the whole story, yet the very invention of it stresses his desire to break free from the binds of dialectical reasoning by telling a simple, supposedly factual story or myth. Thus Socrates must now interpret, together with his interlocutor, the dialogue that Socrates retells as though it were an oracle; that is, he must take it as not his own but rather the other's word that is utterly independent of him even though he spells it out.

This oracular or orally communicated and "heard" story, which is an account of the invention of writing, is paradoxically represented as a written conversation that assimilates what is "heard" with the very source of Greek book wisdom—the Egyptian gods. The interlocutors in the speech that Socrates retells are Theuth (Thoth) and Thamus (Ammon), who stand for the old political division between Lower Egypt (Theuth is from Naucratis) and the triumphant region of Upper Egypt (Thamus is from the capital of Thebes).[4] Theuth is the one who *invents* number, calculation, geometry, astronomy, draughts, dice, and above all, writing, which is the way to present a concept graphically through signs. In contrast, Thamus is the one who *judges*, thus fulfilling one of the most important functions of the king, namely, the ability to tell right from wrong. Despite the fact that Theuth appears to be subordinate to Thamus, they complement each other: the one, Theuth, produces works of art, and in this way assigns being to what does not yet exist (by nature); the other, Thamus, discriminates between what is produced, judging it as either harmful or useful, and thereby grants or refuses it a place in the order of what properly exists. Here, as also in epic poetry, the (skillful) doer does not judge, and the (critical) teller does not produce. The two are independent, yet need each other.

Theuth presents Thamus with the invention of writing as a "cure" for fading memory and lack of wisdom.[5] Theuth takes the invention, the scratches, scribbles, lines, and letters, to be a "science" (*mathēma*), whereas Thamus understands it as an "art" (*tekhnē*). The two designations do not need to be in contradiction, however, because science in antiquity is knowledge that can be communicated, taught, and learned—and teaching and learning are precisely the purpose of writing—while art is a skill that can enhance or complement one's natural capacity, including the capacity to teach and learn.

Theuth's motivation for inventing new devices and giving them to humans is goodwill, or literally, "goodmind" (*eunoia*), a conscious intention to provide a good for the benefit of others. (In this respect, Theuth is similar to Prometheus.) Yet it is precisely because of this good intention that Theuth, who is not a judge, does the opposite. He *misjudges* the purpose of letters and writing (*grammata*). Such misapprehension concerning the real purpose of an invention appears to be a common feature of art in antiquity. Indeed, even if the inventor has a (good and laudable) purpose in mind, the artwork itself, either as an imitation or an improvement of nature, belongs to becoming. Because of this, art can neither grasp nor adequately reproduce the good, which pertains to being and is properly disclosed and justified through dialectically constructed knowledge and discriminatory judgment. Art qua invention inevitably misses its target. Therefore the doer, the inventor or artisan, needs a spectator who can judge and appreciate what is invented.

According to Plato, being is a synthesis of sameness and otherness: being is the other insofar as it is other to what only *has* being by participating in it, and being is the same insofar as it does not change into anything else either in time or in an atemporal logical sequence. Being is represented for humans through and by a discursive and argumentative account, or *logos*, and bears features both of difference from what is other than being and of sameness in its identity with itself and its dialogical transmission. First, with regard to the human capacity to stretch everything out in time or thinking, being is represented in memory (*mnēmē*):

memory must retain and preserve what *was* and the essence, "what," of what was and still is. Second, the correct account or knowledge of being comes from oneself, from the "inside" (*endothen*), thereby making one wise, which occurs in communication and being-together (*synoysia*) with others—in dialogue. And third, one who has the right account of being is also capable of putting it into a discursive form of thought and argument, and is thus able to defend and clarify being by means of dialectic in its relations to the existent.[6]

The judge does not invent the rule according to which a deed is judged, and the artist or doer is subordinated to the judge or teller. Separating becoming from being, Plato likewise separates the two actors, the artist and the judge. Yet Socrates empties himself in order to accept the oracle of the mythological dialogue between Theuth and Thamus. In this way, Socrates is able to embrace both being and becoming, not just by establishing the superiority of the being (also represented as the good, the king, the judge, the teller) over the becoming (the craftsman, the producer, the doer), but also by bringing them into communication with each other. Only by making the two interact and recognize each other in dialogue does it become possible to conceive of the advantages and disadvantages of each project. Thamus/Ammon utters his judgment about writing through Socrates, who empties himself for that judgment just as the poet empties himself in order to become a transmitter or flute of the divine.[7]

The scratched lines of letters or *grammata* are incapable of adequately representing or speaking about being. The reason for this is that the cure and device invented for memory betrays itself in its own purpose insofar as it is not a recipe for memory proper (*mnēmē*), which actually comes from "inside" the self and stores being. Rather, what is memorized in writing stands for something "outside," for an artfully constructed but still unreliable source within becoming. It is a physical imitation that does not imitate what is thought, but only what is said. In its futile hope that *verba volant, scripta manent*—words flee, writing stays—writing can nevertheless only be a reminder (*hypomnēsis*), which is but the appearance of wisdom and not knowledge proper. Such a reminder knows without understanding, and thus results not in the recollection of a memory but in the dissipation of being and knowledge into oblivion.[8]

Besides, writing makes it difficult to communicate with the other, to explain and clarify what one understands, both to the other and to oneself. Dialogical oral speech closely follows being insofar as being is present and reproduced for humans in becoming. Such speech is a living and ensouled logos, yet it is rendered mute and monological through its written imitation (*eidōlon*) or "idol": it is the copy of a copy, a double imitation of what is.

Moreover, writing is stiff and immovable: nothing in it can be changed once it is produced and published. It cannot even clarify or explain itself. Writing is thus a deadening of oral, live speech. Writing is always and forever the same without any chance of becoming other than it is. It cannot change, and in its unchangeability it is *literally* precise. Yet such precision is less precise than so-called "sloppy" oral speech, for oral speech can always explain itself even through grammatically incomplete and rhetorically flawed interrupted sentences. Being petrified, writing cannot *defend* itself, and it does not know when to speak or when to remain silent.[9] Silence, moreover, is not simply a privation of speech, but a momentary suspension of that which brings speech back into an understanding of and with the other. A written speech or "woven" text (*textus* means "woven" in Latin) always speaks, but always says the same thing. It is therefore mute and incapable of changing or becoming other in order to explain itself beyond what has already and forever been said.

In a similar way, de Maistre argues that even a simple oral *conversation* (to which for him *entretien*, or guided oral philosophical dialogue, is far superior) surpasses a written one (a "book") because, unlike the written text of a book, conversation can embrace a proposition that can be further clarified and supported by other propositions when necessary.[10] Oral conversation, therefore, can present dialogues in which propositions can reply to and welcome critical objections. Such objections, of course, may themselves be propositions, which, unlike a fixed literary text, can address other objections through different propositions that specify or even reject the original claim to the extent that a particular claim may become utterly surprising even to the one who originally advanced and supported it. This ability of conversation to be astonishing and unexpected is reproduced and imitated in the genre of commentary that makes a text speak and say what it does not seem to say, and that the text can only say—to its surprise—once it is brought back to oral conversation. Moreover, oral conversation has a remarkable ease and fluency that a composed text does not possess; it always allows for interruption, intervention, and interrogation—for the real discussion of a point—and for listening to and hearing the other. In this respect, de Maistre's unwritten conversation is opposed to its written fixation. The ease of conversation is what makes it so enjoyable and engaging. In contrast, writing cannot accommodate the real other, and the voice of the other is often uncomfortable and unwelcome in written dialogue. The other's voice is not heard and is therefore lacking in writing. The other is inevitably omitted and disregarded by the single demiurgic consciousness of monological written speech.

And finally, a written text cannot interrupt—and thus support—itself in an ongoing conversation, even in a written dialogue. There is a great deal of irony, which is also self-irony, in Plato's use of interruption insofar as he always transcribes an *oral* dispute into *writing*, whether these are the prepared speeches of the Sophists or Socrates' unpredictable dialectical interventions. Even if the interruption is not staged and calculated to address a particular problem or unmask fallacious argumentative techniques, interruption in written dialogue is still only an imitative substitution for spontaneous oral interruption, which guides dialogue.

Gadamer says that modern thinking has two sources that are often combined in various ways.[11] One is Enlightenment, which considers all events from the point of view of a universal Reason, one single unified logos whose inevitable unwrapping in the physical and social world presents itself as progress. The other is Romanticism, which rejects the totalizing claims of Reason and stresses the uniqueness of each individual, literary work, epoch, and culture, thus turning to the production and clarification of multiple and multiplying logoi. Enlightenment looks to the future in search of answers, which it orders within a science-like enterprise. Romanticism looks at the past, where it locates the now lost truth that is inaccessible to us moderns, and so is primarily interested in tradition. If, furthermore, as Michael Gasparov observes, there are thinkers who tend to simplify the world by creating theories and explanations and those who tend to complicate it by creating counterexamples and new meanings, then one might say that the former are the Enlightenment thinkers and the latter are Romantics.

It has been said that philosophy, from Plato through modernity, is logocentric. No doubt both dialectic and dialogue are logocentric insofar as both have recourse to logos. The critique of logocentrism is itself a form of Romanticism. It is a critique that considers only a singular and fixed meaning of logos that it ascribes to Enlightenment. Logos as Reason is understood in the tradition of Enlightenment primarily as self-transparent, discursive, monological reasoning that constructs its own objects through reason's immanent structures. Of all the philosophical terms, logos is perhaps the most elusive, the most difficult to grasp, and is almost impossible to translate because logos needs itself to clarify itself as speech and thinking in and by speech and thinking. As such, it is "said in many ways" and may mean speech, reason, argument, reasoning, definition, or relation.

Logos permeates all reasoning; it *is* reasoning. Logos alone makes it possible to express thought both systematically as dialectic and conversationally as dialogue, and allows humans to communicate and reach out to the other. Without logos, nothing can be said or thought. The very critique of logos is self-referential: it rejects logos by means of logos itself. Because of this, the critique of logos is performatively self-contradictory and self-canceling because, if it were carried out successfully, it would render *any* critique and *any* discussion impossible. This is why Plato warns against the sophistic misery of logos-hating, or "misology," which arises from resentment of being betrayed by treacherous Sophistic reasoning, which in turn makes one distrustful of any logos or reasoning.[12]

Oral dialogue appears to be the very *conditio humana*, whereas written dialogue is a literary genre, a form that implicitly suggests what can and cannot be said. Writing down oral dialogues was already a widespread practice in Plato's time, but for Plato it became *the* genre of philosophizing. However, writing down an oral speech in an attempt to preserve what is said and save it from the non-being of oblivion inevitably changes the speech by substituting an oral dialogical logos with a written one that has its own—dialectical—logic, and thus is a *different* logos.

Philosophy, both "ancient" and "modern," is then writing-oriented, "grammatocentric" or "graphocentric," rather than "logocentric." With and after Plato, philosophy cannot think for itself, cannot think at all, without writing. With a sad sense of irony, Plato must use writing in order to present his philosophy, which cannot altogether be fitted into writing or written dialectic, or remain outside of its written fixation, either, which is a fixation both in the physical and pathological senses.

Ricoeur criticizes Derrida for having missed the proper relation between writing and speaking: "To hold, as Derrida does, that writing has a root distinct from speech and that this foundation has been misunderstood due to our having paid excessive attention to speech, its voice, and its logos, is to overlook the grounding of both modes of the actualization of discourse in the dialectical constitution of discourse."[13] However, in his criticism, Ricoeur himself reverses the relationship between writing and oral speech, because for him discourse is fully and properly present only in written language. Discourse, which for Ricoeur is not dialogical but dialectical in the Hegelian sense, presupposes the dialectic of "distanciation" and "appropriation." Distanciation is a "cultural estrangement" that must be overcome by the hermeneutical and cultured "appropriation" of a text, making it "one's own" in writing and reading. Only in this way, according to Ricoeur, is cultural distance both dialectically suppressed and preserved.[14] The implicit presupposition behind Ricoeur's *written* discourse on discourse is that only writing can become sublime and cultured, whereas its origin as oral speech is base and uncultivated. This is why "the fate of discourse is delivered over to *littera*, not to *vox*."[15] Yet, contra Derrida and Ricoeur, writing and oral speech are not mutually independent communicative modes; neither does writing dialectically supersede oral speech. Writing is an inevitably deficient misappropriation of what is primarily and initially oral. Moreover, oral speech *per se* is not dialectical, because dialectic becomes possible only as a systematic reflection on oral dialogue.

Portrait of a Word. Put into a rigid form incapable of self-defense, written speech, which was originally intended to be a simple record of oral speech, requires interpretation and an interpreter or community of interpreters who can bring what has been written back into live discourse. Written signs, however, are immovable and inflexible and are therefore incapable of self-explanation and self-clarification, which is one of the main reasons for Plato's preferring oral speech over and against writing in his *Seventh Letter*.[16] If a consistent interpretation of a written text is only *an* interpretation, then it can always differ from the author's intended meaning. Yet the *mens auctoris*, the author's intended interpretation of his own text, is itself only *an* interpretation, especially if the text is a dialogue in which the author attempts to reduce himself to being only *a* voice that either allows the other to speak (in dramatic dialogue) or allows the argument to unwrap itself (in dialectical philosophical dialogue). For this reason, restoring the initially intended meaning of a text by reading it might not be the ultimate hermeneutical task.

Writing (*graphê*) is also astonishingly similar to painting (*zōgraphia*), because to write is to draw the portrait of a word. Both show a now absent (dead) object as living, but when one asks a question, the semblance remains solemnly silent. Written speeches speak as if they were thinking, but when the reader inquires about them, they always say the same thing. In this case, "saying the same thing" amounts to "keeping silent" in a perplexing and often embarrassing privation of speech. Being always the same, written speeches are destitute of productive otherness, which has to be brought in by those who read and interpret what is written. The interpreter of a written text for the most part fails to apprehend what was originally said and substitutes it with a new meaning. One tends to see and read (in and out of the text) what one already implicitly presupposes and has in mind. In other words, written logoi lack a *live* logos and can only retain its petrified residue.[17]

Live "ensouled" speech, however, can be transmitted by those who were present while it was still alive and heard it before it was written down. As the *Anonymous Prolegomena* suggest, instead of writing speeches, it is better to leave pupils who are the "live and living speeches" that can explain and defend themselves.[18] Pythagoras and Socrates act in exactly this way, leaving no written speeches but only like-minded disciples capable of communicating both their teachings and their oral speeches, doing so not dogmatically but aporetically in and through ongoing discussions. In this way, the oral logos of a founder is transmitted not by being rigidly fixed in written form—perhaps mnemonically in the form of shorter sayings—but by remaining alive and thus capable of being developed further, always staying the same yet becoming different through discussion. The oral word is still alive in "living speeches" or disciples. Such speeches live through Plato as a disciple of Socrates, and through the followers of the Pythagorean, Heraclitean, and Parmenidean traditions, which are all present in Plato's philosophy. As a process and activity, writing is solitary and requires solitude, whereas oral dialogue, which is continued in and through students, always occurs with others and presupposes a multiplicity of speakers.

Perhaps Plato attempted to offer a compromise between being and becoming. As the *Anonymous Prolegomena* continues to explain, "Plato strove to imitate the divine, and in choosing to write he let a greater good prevail over a lesser evil. For god has made some parts of his creation invisible, namely, all incorporeal beings, angels, souls, and intellects, etc., yet some other parts are subject to our perception and are visible, such as heavenly bodies and the world of becoming. So Plato too has passed on some of his ideas in writing and some in an unwritten form, like incorporeal entities, imperceptible to the senses. . . . Therefore, to show his friendship with the divine even in this, he endeavored to imitate it, as friends will try to imitate each other."[19] Writing thus imitates the bodily, whereas what is unwritten and oral imitates what is thinkable. Because for Plato the bodily is itself an imitation of the intelligible, writing is an imitation of an imitation and hence always fails.

As the drawing of a word, writing originally represents the word as a pictogram, and, in a more developed way, as a hieroglyph.[20] In hieroglyphic writing (e.g., Egyptian or Chinese), a sign directly stands as a picture for a concept in non-discursive thinking, which grasps a thought without any chain of reasoning or argument—that is, not dialectically. Writing and reading move through written texts discursively and gradually, step by step. But if Plato is right in holding that being cannot be known discursively (if it can be known at all), then it cannot be approached through a step-by-step dialectical movement or argumentation, and it cannot be properly represented, written down, or read.

The pictured word thus attempts to stand for something—that which is—for which it cannot stand. Therefore, such a word represents what cannot be represented and thus inevitably ends up representing something else. In such signed writing, a physical thing—a hieroglyph—points at a notion, bearing only the hint of a thought as though it were disclosing it yet at the same time veiling its meaning through something that is distinct from what is meant. The portrait of a word is present, thematized, and seen. But what it points to is never fully seen or thematized.

Greek linear writing, on the contrary, does not transmit a concept but rather an already discursive and well ordered (dialectical and logical) representation, both in its expression through discursive thinking and through its utterance in dialogical speech. Such a representation is not complete but instead is always yet to be completed and gathered from single and seemingly isolated fragments.[21] In other words, phonetic writing is a representation of a representation, a double imitation of being.

Hieroglyphic writing is based on the ineradicable difference between discursive thinking (*logos*), which is a process that is partial and incomplete, and non-discursive thinking (*nous*), which is an act that is also the thinking of being. Phonetic linear writing, in contrast, is rooted in the opposition between writing and discursive speaking or thinking in and through speech. In both cases, however, writing as an art (*tekhnē*) belongs to the sphere of doing and production (*poiēsis*), whose end is outside of and different from itself. As production, the art of writing therefore ends, on the one hand, in dialectical thinking, which runs discursively through correct and systematically well-ordered thoughts as part of an established argument. On the other hand, the art of writing ends in dialogical speech and the expression of thought in a sequence of signs.

Yuri Olesha says in *Envy*, an early modernist novel of the twentieth century, that people are always surrounded by small inscriptions that silently appear in the most unexpected places.[22] In modernity, the whole of the perceptible world is appropriated as "signed," whereby a sign as label is attached to every object and mental state. Moreover, a sign is also a form of inscription that is initially produced by people who do not want to be forgotten and hence render themselves visible and readable through such signs. The reading of an inscription must be voiced, which means that small inscriptions should first be rendered internally (through reading), and then externally (by discussing them with others and thus restoring them in oral speech). Then the inscriptions must be rendered internally again (by gathering the meaning of what is said or the name that is supposed to be remembered).

Inscriptions cover much of the buildings and temple walls at Delphi, where the inscriptions themselves are historical documents, like the graffiti from the seventeenth and eighteenth centuries that covers the lime walls of the Egyptian temple of Dendur and the bell tower of the Strasbourg Cathedral. The inalienable and insatiable human desire to leave signs and to produce texts (e.g., by publishing books) appears to be an expression of the profound need to communicate with the imaginable addressee and projected other who is not yet present and who will remember the writer and addresser, and thus save her from the "futility of oblivion" (to use Hannah Arendt's words). Addressing the not yet present other, such inscriptions have *sua fata*; they live and die, become famous and fall into oblivion. The originally selfless inscriptions are forced into existence by being capitalized, advertised, and imposed onto the others' immediate and intimate surroundings by being brought to everyone's—and hence no one's—attention. This makes small inscriptions big, but at the same time renders each small inscription even smaller, unnoticeable, unreadable, almost obliterated, and incapable of addressing anyone. Small inscriptions, which do not fit into a dialogical exchange, defy and cancel themselves.

The Precision of Oral Dialogue. Writing cannot be other than it is, and it is always an *artificial* construction and therefore a matter of art. It is produced in such a way as to reproduce and fix a story or an established argument with all possible psychological, factual, or logical precision. And yet, renewable and unsystematic oral dialogue has its own measure of precision, different from the precision of a written text. The precision of writing is that of protracted deliberation, minute details, and exact references. Oral dialogue does not provide all of the accurate citations, such as page numbers and years of publication, but it does—or at least can—provide a very strict meaning, even if it is not fully thematizable, namely that of the personal other.

The written fixation of renewable oral exchange attempts to overcome the seeming haphazardness of oral speech and make dialogue either serve the ends of a pre-established plot (as literary dialogue) or those of a precise, science-like methodical and dialectical discourse (as philosophical dialogue). Oral dialogue, however, which moves freely from one topic to another and is thus easily exchanged between speakers, is more precise than an established argument that can meticulously gather and reproduce hundreds of steps in the correct order of reasoning.

Oral dialogue is more precise, in its own way, than written dialogue and even dialectic, because, first, one can always inquire over again in a conversation. One can ask for the clarification of a point, for further elaboration, and for a response to one's criticism, moving on to other details and unexpected turns in the discussion. The precision of imprecise dialogue thus consists in its ability to clarify what is said again and again, often by interrupting the interlocutor. If what is said is not clear, then it can always be further questioned and clarified in oral dialogue. Any unexpected objection can be answered, and any unanticipated turn can be reacted to. And second, the main point or central idea in oral exchange can always be explained briefly when necessary, "in a couple of words." A written text (e.g., that of the dialogue) possesses the dialectical literal precision of minute references, whereas oral dialogical speech possesses precision of meaning and the possibility of a concise clarification.

Oral speech is precise not literally (according to the "letter") but in terms of its meaning (its "spirit"), which, however, is subject to revision over and over in any oral dialogue and throughout the generations of its tradition. Since the very "life of the mind" consists in debate and dialogical discussion, which is both a starting point and the point of destination, there is no need for an ultimate or definitively established speech that would become the standard reference.

Written logos, especially that of dialectic and written philosophical dialogue, strives to be universal by establishing valid arguments. Yet it is the renewable and always seemingly different oral logos that is universal, for by belonging to everyone who participates in an oral discussion it can always continue unwrapping, clarifying, and rendering more precise an idea or personal other.

A written text can be helpful as a reminder when memory begins to fade and fail.[23] The paradigmatic written text, then, is a set of loosely organized notes scribbled as a reminder of what is heard and is meant for oneself, not for the other, so that one might restore what was said after a period of time. Still, as time passes, even the writer might fail to recognize the meaning of what was said, and when the writer dies, that meaning is most probably lost even if the text is preserved and published. Only the renewable conversation can save what is said, and this only for a brief moment in conversation. The eternal truth of a story, an argument, or personal other thus lives only in the transience of oral dialogue.

The Authority of Writing: The Death of the Oracle. What if writing is a way of, and toward, self-cognition? Perhaps to know oneself is to write oneself out, to spell oneself out for the other, but equally also for oneself as the other, and in this way to finally understand what one wants or intends to say? One of the major theses in Schleiermacher's hermeneutic is that, by reading a text, a reader can—and should—understand the writer *better* than she understands herself. In this sense, the reader has an advantage over the writer. In Gadamer's critical interpretation, this thesis (which is traced back by Bollnow to a note in Kant concerning Plato [KrV B370]) means that to understand a text is to reconstruct the process of its creation and thus understand something that the writer herself was trying to understand but could not. In this way, the reader is in a better position to disclose the "inner form" of a text and find out what it really "means" (*meint*).[24]

However, a writer can also be his own reader. The writer is in the same position as anyone else of being able to understand and interpret his own text, especially when, as Plato argues, the writer forgets what he wrote, which happens over time. Furthermore, even if a given reading follows certain established or implicit principles of interpretation and is not just an instance where "anything goes," it is possible to provide *many different yet consistent interpretations of the same text.* Thought (what is understood) and oral speech (what is said) may never fully fit into writing insofar as what is written is fixed and as such can never exhaust all of its possible intended and even unintended meanings. But the inexpressible "surplus" of oral speech does not have to be taken as a hidden meaning that lies "behind" or "beneath" the literal one, as an esoteric subtext that is only accessible to privileged readers.

In *Persecution and the Art of Thinking,* Leo Strauss argues that all philosophers at all times do the same work—that of thinking, and hence they form "a class by themselves."[25] Yet all philosophers are always being persecuted in one way or another. Therefore, as philosophers, they must think freely, but as oppressed citizens of a particular political order they cannot do so. Because of this, philosophers as a "class" must work out a specific technique of writing. For Strauss, any philosophical text is "exoteric" on its surface and is meant for a general reader, but it is "esoteric" in its real message, which is meant for the careful and philosophically minded reader who can read "between the lines." Thus philosophical writing assumes that "thoughtless men are careless readers, and that only thoughtful men are careful readers. An author, therefore, who wishes to address only thoughtful men has but to write in such a way that only a very careful reader can detect the meaning of his book."[26] Of course, one might ask whether one should read "between the lines" of this and other claims of Strauss too, in which case the distinction between "exoteric" and "esoteric" becomes self-defeating.

The distinction between "exoteric" and "esoteric" unduly assimilates the former to public and the latter to private use, such that one can only be free privately and never in the public sphere. For Strauss philosophy is inevitably "esoteric" as a method of self-protection: those who deviate from mainstream thought are persecuted by being punished and ostracized—and in a truly liberal society "esoteric" writing makes it possible to uncover the utmost hidden beauty of a text, which is discovered as a result of careful (and never easy) reading. But if a philosopher is inevitably persecuted, then why write at all? Is it because the sacred is given in the form of a text such that one must perhaps imitate the divine; or is persecution due to the vain hope of being read by imaginary "thoughtful men" who will continue the same perennial philosophical pursuit of reading and writing? If philosophy can be performed only by reading between the lines and thus excavating the hidden meaning and address of a text, then doing philosophy is impossible without texts. If this is the case, philosophy is nothing but reading written philosophical texts, and, contrary to the claim that philosophers are always engaged in free thought, thinking without reading is impossible and meaningless. However, for Strauss and his readers, philosophy can never be thinking that is free of texts: philosophy for him is possible only by thinking about texts. Philosophy as "esoteric," then, must necessarily be both written and read. If, however, thinking is to be free, then it must also be free of texts. For Strauss, writing is what liberates philosophers from persecution, but in fact writing oppresses thought by binding it to interpretation.

Thus, if philosophy has anything to do with free thought, it cannot be esoteric and cannot be a philosophy of "reading between the lines." Rather, philosophy must be a free dialogical discussion that is accessible and open to everyone. Any meaning is in principle accessible and understandable to any reader, such that no one (not even a Straussian) has a privileged position in relation to a given text. Different yet equally plausible interpretations are possible if the understanding of a text is meant to be polyphonic and dialogical, and not strictly logical or dialectical and oriented toward establishing a single true thesis that results from reading and interpreting a text. What a text really *means* may not be *uni*form—that is, disclose only one intended meaning.

Moreover, Schleiermacher's thesis that the reader in principle understands and *knows* the other better than the other understands himself implies that writing cannot be a way of self-cognition. But perhaps it is only a striving toward self-understanding that remains incomplete? Or maybe the writer comes to understand himself through a long process of discursive reasoning similar to that of dialectic that also includes incorrect steps and mistaken arguments, whereas the reader is saved from the pain of such a journey and can see the ultimate result, distilled into writing? Yet reading is equally a discursive process of collecting (with luck) the (or a) meaning of what is undergone and "what the text really means," which can only be ascertained at the very end. The writer's understanding of his text—but not of himself—is in principle equal to that of any other reader, and thus when reading his own text the author is only *a* reader and does not have an advantage in interpreting and construing his own text. Because of this, the produced written text is "before" the reader, which means that it is also "before" its own writer. Thus a written text always (hermeneutically, not temporally) precedes efforts to read and understand it.

Reading a text may be not only a solitary and monological reflection but also a joint hermeneutical deliberation within a *dialogical* community that reads, and especially rereads, a text. Writing presupposes reading; the Greek word for "to read" is *anagignōskō*, "to recognize," which means that what is written reminds one of the original and now forgotten sense of what was said. As I said earlier, it is likely that the mimes of Sophron influenced Plato's elaboration of the genre of dramatic and dialectical written dialogue. It is also likely that the mimes were written not for the stage but for *reading* only. Likewise, Plato's dialogues were written not for the stage but for reading, which in antiquity meant being read aloud with and for others. Even if a text does not contain all of the meanings it might imply, its being read allows for the possibility of discovering new and different interpretations of a text. Qua readers, the members of a hermeneutical community are equal and independent even though each one may reasonably claim to have a better interpretation according to the accepted hermeneutical rules of reading and interpretation. Since everyone within an interpretative community has equal access to the interpretation of a text, and since the text cannot explicitly spell out everything it might be interpreted to say, the text therefore becomes primary to any interpretation. Paradoxically, a text that cannot say anything beyond what it does say and can still say much more once it becomes central to an interpretive community. Such a text thus becomes "sacred."

A "sacred" written text is established as a decisive authority by its readers. Any "primary" text becomes "sacred" for its later tradition of followers, interpreters, and commentators. In such a text nothing should be changed, and what is written should be accepted in its entirety. A sacred text is always already and forever given. It becomes the ultimate source of reference capable of providing all possible interpretations of the world. What is considered reality, then, can only be accessible through what is written and frozen into *the* text, which is inevitably interpreted and then distorted through the prism of writing or "culture" as it has arisen based on the foundation of a sacred text.

Every text, every written speech, must have an author. Even though a text exists (hermeneutically) *before* its author, because it is produced by an author it must at the same time also exist (temporally) *after* the author. A written text cannot temporally precede its author because it cannot meaningfully be spoken of before it is actually written. Therefore a text and its author have to be coequal and coeval, as it were, in order to level or suspend their respective "before" and "after." Because a text is properly atemporal before it is actually produced and written, a sacred text must in a sense be *its own author*. This author is the one who always reveals him-/her-/itself while at the same time unavoidably hiding him-/her-/itself, always being discovered and missed in various ways by the interpreters and loyal readers of a written text.

Every written narrative, even if it is intended to be merely an "objective" retelling of things that have happened and the words that were said, nevertheless inescapably deviates from oral speech. Writing distorts oral dialogue because oral dialogue is communication, and written dialogue is a solitary monological written speech that is self-defeating in its very purpose. Even if one speaks to oneself, one speaks to oneself as the other. A genuine dialogue can only be a spontaneous oral exchange that presents itself without reference to an external authority—the authority of an author or a primary written text. A written dialogue mediates between oral dialogue and dialectic, and also *imitates* oral dialectic along with all of the twists and turns of its movement. The writer *already* knows what the result of the discussion will and should be, and if the dialogue itself comes to the wrong conclusion or remains inconclusive, then the author can preserve this inconclusiveness, which may either depict the motion of dialectical thought or entice the reader to think the argument through even further—perhaps from a different perspective. In the latter case an inconclusive argument may contain a hint toward a possible solution or simply be at a complete loss. But if a written representation of dialogue distorts what was said in oral speech, then the written inevitably (even if unintentionally) always misses the point. If the author is conscious of this, as Plato is, then a written presentation of oral dialogue can be only protreptic and ironic, and never takes itself too seriously. Any philosophy that occurs as a systematic fixation of oral philosophizing must therefore also be ironic.

In the *Phaedrus*, Socrates ironically reproaches the "new," enlightened, and sophisticated writers for being "wise." In the context of that discussion, this means being "rhetorically wise" or strong in persuasion, in "making the weakest speech the strongest."[27] The "new" draw their wisdom from writings whose purpose, however, is merely to be reminders of things past. Writing is authoritative. It commands authority by being made public—by being published and thereby publicized. The incapacity on the part of writing-oriented thinking to listen to oral speech and understand oracular speech (*logos mantikos*; particularly the oracle of Ammon against writing uttered through Socrates) results in the death of the spoken word.

This is also the death of the oracle. Living the oracle demands a readiness on the part of its hearers to unreflectively accept the authority of anybody or anything (even an illiterate tree or rock) to speak sincerely and truthfully, even if such speech is often not understood. The death of the oracle means that its authority is replaced by an ongoing written interpretation of what is from then on forever given as a sacred text.

Once writing gains full advantage over oral speech, the oracle is no longer needed and is allowed to die. The oracle is dead in and for the written world. One might even say that modernity can be characterized by the death of the oracle for both the Enlightenment and Romanticism. The oracle is not heard because it is no longer questioned. Only interpretations, oral as well as written, make sense and still survive in writing-oriented speech, but such speech is itself an interpretation of past oracles that fell silent long ago.[28]

The "wise" and the "new" whom Socrates has in mind when making his ironic remark are first and foremost the Sophists, who are "wise" in writing and strong in composing beautiful persuasive speeches. In doing so, however, Socrates is not original, for there is an undeniable similarity between his philippics against writing in the *Phaedrus* and the speech of the Sophist Alcidamas, entitled *On Those Who Write Their Speeches, or on Sophists.*[29] Writing against Isocrates (who studied with Prodicus and Gorgias and listened to Socrates), Alcidamas argues that it is not even proper to call written speeches "speeches" because they are only inert images, appearances, and imitations (*eidōla, skhēmata, mimēmata*) of live speeches. Live speech for Alcidamas, however, is not just any speech but a publicly pronounced extemporaneous one, which thus has to be grammatically perfect and rhetorically beautiful. Live speech is preferable to written speech (which was meant to be memorized and presented on a certain occasion), because writing takes too much time to compose and cannot change according to an unpredictable new situation (in a political gathering or in court), whereas oral improvised speech is much more flexible and requires memorizing only a few major moves and arguments. Moreover—and this same argument appears in Plato's critique of writing—just as bronze statues imitate living bodies, and just as the bronze images are beautiful yet utterly useless, so too are written speeches: they cannot talk back, cannot reply, object, disagree, or continue a conversation. Oral speech is pronounced from and with understanding; being "ensouled" and "alive," it keeps pace with the circumstances in which it is set. For this reason, oral speech is similar to living and ensouled bodies, whereas writing is only a lifeless and frozen imitation of oral speech devoid of any activity beyond the interpretative efforts of its readers.

Both Alcidamas and Plato agree that, although written speech embraces dialectical methods, it is itself an *artificial* reproduction as either an imitation or a reconstruction of oral speech. Therefore, writing inevitably betrays live speech.[30]

However, Alcidamas' critique appears paradoxical and performatively self-contradictory, which he recognizes, insofar as he criticizes writing in and by means of writing. Since Alcidamas is himself a Sophist, his speech must unavoidably target itself. He informs us that he is not opposed to writing as such, but only to the (professional and hence paid) writing of ready-made public speeches that cannot compete with incomparably more flexible extemporaneous speeches. Alcidamas, however, does not resolve the problem of the relation of speech and writing in general, but instead leaves his own logos as a carefully, beautifully, and purposely composed written speech.

Being written and thus made possible, writing against writing makes itself impossible. This is also the case with my own present writing against writing. A solution to this paradox is that writing is an activity that, if it is not altogether rejected, must at least be severely limited through self-criticism or critical reflection, which establishes the limits of writing by revealing its purposes. To be sure, writing against writing does not advocate illiteracy, for literacy is indeed important, though it has a limited scope. A proper critique of writing must come from and within oral speech. Yet oral speech cannot be preserved long enough; it dissipates over time and is lost to oblivion if it is not conserved by written speech. The purpose of writing as "mnemonic" is then primarily historical: writing serves to preserve things and events from the past, saving them from the "futility of oblivion," but does not provide access to things as they are, to being.

In the *Seventh Letter*, Plato goes even further in his critique of writing. There he stresses not only that oral dialogical speech can never fit the Procrustean couch of speech frozen into writing, but that even oral discursive speech is not flexible enough to adequately express being, which can only be grasped in a sudden momentary insight of non-discursive, hence non-dialectical and non-dialogical, thought.[31] There is thus an ineradicable obstacle and hindrance for anybody who intends to write: writing, being itself only an imitation of oral speech, is as though "twice" or doubly inflexible and unfit to represent what is thought, because even oral speech, which is spoken and uttered, cannot adequately express what is understood in thought. For this reason, Plato prefers not to leave any writings about the matters discussed in the Academy and keeps such orally debated teachings accessible to everyone yet separate from his own writings, leaving them unwritten.[32]

Thus the writing-based authority of *les hommes de lettres* obliterates the oracle because the oracle undermines writing and is potentially dangerous to it. (In antiquity there were numerous stories of corruption of the literate interpreters of the oracle, namely the priests, who, being bribed, would provide the required interpretations.) Indeed, the oracle is unexpected. Nobody can predict, usurp, or dispose of oracular speech or the proper time (*kairos*) at which the oracle will resume speaking. Yet the "wise," "new," sophisticated, and writing-minded "moderns" accept and recognize authority by carefully discriminating between *who* speaks and *whence* what is said or written derives. The *who* and *whence* determine whether the literate others will recognize and accept the authority of an interpretation of a written text. The oracle becomes mute once it is written down and usurped by an entire class of those who are letter-oriented and who thus appropriate the privilege of interpreting what is pronounced. The reference to the "whence" of writing and a succession of authoritative interpretations of scholars and illustrious writers treats writing as autonomous and thus completely disregards the unsophisticated truthfulness of the oracle's free oral speech, no matter who utters it.

Why Write? Is there any purpose in writing? Clearly, writing against writing is performatively self-contradictory. Yet both Plato and Alcidamas pronounce their verdict against writing by writing. Not only does Plato reject writing *in* writing and *by means of* writing, but he himself continues to write even after his own devastating critique, rather than simply remaining silent. Writing "after writing" may be understood as an overcoming of writing in writing and by the very act of writing, a *sui generis* dialectical self-cancellation and a return to oral and inquisitive logos, which is now meant to be *both* dialogical and dialectical.

A critique of writing is always difficult, not only because it seems self-contradictory to criticize writing in and by writing. Such a critique is either ironic, or suggests a new ("modernistic," "poetic," "deconstructive," or other) use of writing, or points toward a self-overcoming of writing or its "sublation" by not writing. One might say that writing inevitably abandons and even betrays what is. If being (as both being there and being what one is) is personal and dialogical, and hence becomes apparent through the oral speech of dialogue, then it is constantly renovated and expressed in oral communication, but fails such recurrence in textual retention and written transmission. Writing, as an attempt to preserve dialectic, is monoconscious and monological. Hence dialectic is written and monological, whereas dialogue is oral but can be imitated through writing. A philosophical written dialogue also imitates dialectic, which is originally implicit in oral dialogue. Of all the forms of writing, however, written dialogue is a minimal compromise because it imitates, follows, and often reinvents an oral exchange to the closest possible degree, including a dialectical exchange that is originally oral. It is for this reason that Plato chooses the genre of dialogue, which, however, is nevertheless not self-sufficient because even if a written dialogue is considered to be a microcosm, still its source, its meaning and completion, remains beyond writing and thus outside of written dialogue. Written dialogue is monological. To be sure, a written dialogue can induce its oral and dialogical interpretation, but once the tradition of "living speeches" is exhausted, then a written dialogical speech, incapable of "defending itself," will never be able to convey the original concerns, intentions, and conclusions of the originally oral and "ensouled" dialogue now bound into writing.

Thus writing seems incapable of adequately standing in for oral speech, and even less for an understanding of what is. Socrates compares writing to the futile attempt at writing on water with ink and a reed pen.[33] Such written speeches are incapable of helping themselves in either self-explanation or self-defense because that which is—being—cannot be fully thematized either in oral dialogical speech or by discursive dialectical thinking. To write on water is no different from producing the shadow of a shadow.

Perhaps writing is just a (bad) habit? We become addicted to writing and cannot leave it alone. Writing becomes our "second nature" and as such dictates our destiny as humankind. We are taught to read and write because in doing so, we are told, we participate in culture, and only in this way is our culture preserved, such that it becomes a duty to carry on writing. The critique of writing makes us uneasy and is often taken personally, as an offense, because we are what we read, and the criticism of the written is a criticism of our own cultured literate self. Yet our literate "written" identity is based on the *sola scriptura* assumption that everything worth preserving and developing is some kind of a text, including philosophy, which from its very inception is written. Therefore, a critique of writing is also a critique of philosophy as a "project."

The attraction of writing is also accompanied by a vain hope for immortality: the writer anticipates being remembered after he or she is gone, and in this way hopes to secure a personal presence and position in the being of culture—if not in body then at least in name as it is written into the memory of future generations.[34] The deceptive appeal to and hope for a kind of immortality in memory is so appealing that the preservation of an imageless name is preferred over the preservation of an anonymous image. Unlike an anonymous image of no one, a name can be included in a continuing oral discourse and thus become significant through tradition. However, for a writer who is still living, the removed afterlife of nominal survival always remains only a possibility and never an unfulfilled desire. No one knows whose name will be preserved and whose will be forgotten. Furthermore, even if one's name is preserved, as a writer expects it will be, it does not secure being, because being is not in a suspended historical existence against oblivion, but rather in the now of dialogical communication with the other.

Writing is still useful for certain purposes, which, however, have nothing to do with the special access to being through texts that it declares. Writing is valuable for recollections in the form of memoirs that preserve events or speeches from the past. Writing allows one to save arguments in their complexity from disappearing into oblivion along with all of their steps and minute details. This is the "Enlightenment" function of writing: from the time that Sophistical rational justification becomes tantamount to arriving at the truth, it becomes important to say *what* is true, but even more important to say *why* it is true. The imperative is to argue correctly and to keep long dialectical chains of reasoning from forgetfulness, which is better achieved in writing.

In particular, the very arguments against writing, if they themselves were not written down, would soon be forgotten once the succession of "living speeches," disciples and followers, were exhausted and dissipated. It may be better to retain a recollection or a reminder, even if only a faint one, of such discussions. It may be better, therefore, to put such a reminder into writing, which allows for repetition and poring over what is written again and again by discussing it with others or by simply gazing at the text. A live oral dialogue and discussion, in contrast, is unique, irreversible, and unrepeatable. One can always return to the written word in both oral and written discussion, whereas the oral word is transient and momentary, existing and then immediately becoming a fact of the past that will be forgotten if it is not retained in a reminder, either inadvertently or purposefully. Yet as a reminder or set of notes from a scholarly presentation or talk, writing is written mostly for oneself, *ad se ipsum*. In this role, again, writing is meant to cope with forgetting when the memory is overloaded or fails.

Early modern science presupposes that the development of human knowledge is cumulative, implying a constant increase in what is known. If this is the case, then writing helps preserve what has already been discovered in order to pass it on to future generations. Galileo says of writing (in a written dialogue): "But surpassing all stupendous inventions, what sublimity of mind was his who dreamed of finding means to communicate his deepest thoughts to any other person, though distant by mighty intervals of place and time! . . . of speaking to those who are not yet born and will not be born for a thousand or ten thousand years; and with what facility, by the different arrangements of twenty characters upon a page!"[35] The problem with such an understanding of the Enlightenment idea of progress in knowledge is that it makes previous achievements only relative to the present state of knowledge, which itself will inevitably look naïve from the perspective of later generations that do not take much interest in previous knowledge except for historical curiosity. Hence, if there is a constant accumulation of knowledge, then knowledge of "what is" is never complete and its written preservation never allows us to access being in full.

Furthermore, as Alcidamas argues, writing can preserve not only exemplary logoi as dialectical arguments, but also logoi as beautiful rhetorical speeches that are taken as paradigmatic and thus serve as a reference for those who try to produce speeches of equal artistic worth. Therefore writing is central to education insofar as education is based on the imitation and variation of exemplary instances.

Writing is of utter importance, of course, to literature, which produces texts and employs the art of deception—fiction—that shows, as Aristotle famously says,[36] things human not as they were (which is history), but as they might have been. Seeing and reading about how things might have been brings with it the joy of recognizing possibilities in one's own life and familiar people in literary characters. This kind of recognition is what Plato calls "recollection," for it is a recollection not only of knowledge about "what is," but also about how we humans can arrive at it. The recollection in writing of what is already known but is either forgotten or not explicitly formulated, is the work of "memory" broadly speaking, and involves a joy and pleasure of recognition.

For this reason, and because of its incongruence with spontaneous speech, writing should not be taken too seriously, but rather as a game and amusement (*paidia*, as both Alcidamas and Socrates refer to writing). On the one hand, enjoyment is relaxing and should secure rest, the purpose of which, for Aristotle, is restoration for the sake of a serious and meaningful activity.[37] On the other hand, the game of writing strives to attain what cannot be attained in writing, namely, being and live oral speech. Because of this, writing inevitably and always has an ironic touch. As such, writing should be practiced almost without care and nonchalantly as if it were not worthy of effort, as a *sprezzatura*—or at least this should be the impression that it gives. Details and that which is apparently incidental (*parergon*) and an accidental attribute or addition to what is essential in a "work" (*ergon*) should nevertheless be taken seriously, though perhaps not as more important than, the thing itself.[38] This is the case in literature, which, unlike philosophy, does not have to produce theories but must pay attention to detail. What is incidental, then, not only adds something to the whole, but also, by being expressed from a certain perspective, itself tends to become a self-contained work (such as *Parerga* in Schopenhauer) or activity (such as playing, which has no purpose beyond itself).

Playing the game of writing against writing by speaking through Socrates, Plato wants to establish the art of dialectic, which is meant to provide well-being and immortality to humans.[39] Perhaps, though, Plato's ambition is to preserve his own written dialogues as examples for generations of disciples and followers, or at least as writings that would outlive the serious written speeches of the Sophists. Dialectic is oral for Socrates and is written down by Plato. Perhaps writing dialogues is Plato's attempt to provide a durable example of dialectical methods of reasoning. Yet he cannot really accomplish this because dialectic is written, and qua written it cannot grasp the subtlety of live reason and reasoning. Written dialectical dialogue cannot fly; it cannot fully contain live Socratic thinking, which is always exercised in dialogue with others.

The casual and playful character of writing further implies that it should not be considered a professional occupation, but more so a matter of leisure. Leisure is the Latin *otium* or Greek *skholē*, and "scholars" are those who take writing, reading, and research as a game in pursuit of pleasure during their free time. This is the case for writers and scholars from Plato and Strabo through Lavoisier and the nineteenth-century scientists, until science and scholarship became a profession and Weberian "*Beruf*," thereby turning from a "vocation" into a serious business (*negotium*, "non-leisure").

The written becomes meaningful within a self-contained and protracted game of writing as an exercise of one's privacy and freedom. As such, writing is opposed to the amusements of oral symposium, which is drinking accompanied by a common discussion where the interlocutors routinely disagree with and interrupt each other. Plato's attitude toward writing as a private *paidia* later became a recognized practice with the Stoics, including Seneca and Marcus Aurelius, who both wrote personal notes directed to themselves at leisure.

In the discussion of oral speech and writing one might further distinguish, as contemporary linguists do, between the medial and the conceptual in speech. The former stands for the medium and the way of its representation, the latter for its concept.[40] Any monologue is always conceptually written, whether it is medially oral (spoken, represented phonetically) or medially written (printed, represented graphically). A published dialogue (e.g., one of Plato's dialogues), in contrast, is conceptually oral yet medially written. But only live dialogue is both medially and conceptually oral. Only in this case does the way in which speech reveals itself through and to us coincide with the way in which it is conceived as communicative and intersubjective.

Written dialogue strives to reproduce and preserve, and yet always misrepresents, oral dialogue. Oral dialogue, even if it does not intend to, presents live thinking and lets it live in thought, which is often haphazard and not organized dialectically into an argument but is always thought out together with the other. Thinking in oral speech consists in the exchange of discrete yet non-isolated thoughts. Such thinking is dialogical and thus does not fully fit within the systematically constructed and woven monological text of written dialogue. Dialectical, monological, and exclusive of the other yet imitative of oral dialogue, written dialogue out of all genres comes closest to incorporating the dialogical other.

Another way of breaking with the systematic monoconsciousness of writing is its dissolution into a (written) collection of fragments or *aphorisms*, where no thought is given ultimate priority over the others. The form or genre of the "aphorism" is used very differently. It can be a series of short oracular maxims, as those that cover the walls of the temple of Apollo at Delphi, or a collection of *pensées* that come to mind and are preserved as signs of one's "wit." Aphorisms can be loosely related to a topic, as in La Rochefoucauld's *Maximes* and Vauvenargues' *Réflexions et maximes*, or can unwrap a theme (knowledge, science, etc.) from ever-changing perspectives, as in the Platonic *Definitions*, Francis Bacon's *New Organon*, or Wittgenstein's *Philosophical Investigations*. A fragment may be a short text that is either a curious story or anecdote collected along with others, as in Plutarch's *Convivial Questions*, Aulus Gellius' *Noctes Atticae,* or Aelian's *Varia Historia*, or a set of stories arranged thematically with other texts to form a collection on a certain topic, as in Pliny's *Natural History*, Epictetus' *Discourses* on various (mostly moral) subjects, Montaigne's *Essais*, or Nietzsche's *Human, All too Human.* In Schlegel's *Athenaeum* fragments, the genre of the fragment is perfected in its systematic non-systematicity: a fragment *happens*, after which one can only say *scripsi*, I wrote what I wrote, and I purposely leave it written yet unedited, "uncombed," and stylistically imperfect to let it live its own life and speak as a testimony, a trace of a past live thought.

The written representation of thought within a fragment is itself often commented on in another written fragment. A fragment and an aphorism reflect the whole of a thought both in its discreteness and in its entirety—that is, in non-isolation from other thoughts and the context of the discussion. Being mutually independent and complete, different fragments allow for further interpretations that might bring them together into a coherent narrative. Such a narrative, however, can be woven in different ways depending on the cast of dialogical characters and the dialogical situation. Each interpretive version may be independent of any other one, and none follows in a strict manner from a fragment or a collection of fragments. Each fragment, then, is prior to a (re)constructed narrative or argument that binds separate fragments together. The fragment, which exists mostly in written form, is thus a close yet still inadequate representation of a complete but not systematically closed thought. Such thought is not even fully accessible to oral speech, in which thought remains unexpected and renewable and can always be continued in dialogical exchange. Writing fragments or aphorisms is thus a compromise with writing in writing and by means of writing.

Writing, Philosophy, and Lawgiving. Writing thus does not preserve what "is" in its entirety, which may never be accessible, even to oral speech. Writing, however, does preserve what "was," yet only partially. To be sure, history not only preserves things past, but also changes them by interpreting them and "understanding" them; and when they are not available, it makes them up. History always has a narrative component and refers to literary fiction, such as when it invents oral speeches and assigns them to the described characters (e.g., to Pericles by Thucydides), or restores—fills in, according to the mind of the writer—gaps in the understanding of other cultures (e.g., in Herodotus).

One might say that the *duty* of history is to maintain things past, names of people and accounts of events, thus saving them from the *nihil* of oblivion. The names of heroes are retained in epic poetry (e.g., Homer); the names of ancestors are maintained in genealogies (e.g., Hesiod and Thucydides); the names of the known and inhabited parts of the universe are kept in early "histories" (e.g., Hecataeus). All of these records preserve things for historical being from being forgotten. History preserves the names and details of past events without distinguishing between what is important and what is unimportant, simply saving them for and in the collective—originally oral and then written—memory, protecting them from dissipation over generations. For this reason, in its capacity as a reminder, writing is of undeniable importance for history and for preserving long lists of names and events.

However, the "most important" events of history, those that are still alive and influence the lives and bearers of their history, can be left unwritten because they are known (even if their interpretations change) to everyone who lives in and shares that history: a great war, the foundational moment of a republic, someone's travels, scientific discovery. What is considered the "most important" is conceived of as real and as being. But being is beyond the grasp of writing. Being resists being written down. (The Alcidamas/ Plato account preserves—in writing—this attitude toward writing.) One of the "most important" things is law because it brings people together from dispersion and allows them to be a people in a free political state. Because of this, many peoples of antiquity, including the Romans, opposed writing down their laws for a long time.

The concealed fear in writing down and publishing the law is that, if it is written, somebody might, intentionally or unintentionally, change something in the inscription, in the law's written appearance, which in turn might change the law itself. Changing the law is perceived as destroying or irreversibly altering the social and political life of the people, so that not only their past, but also their future—their well-being and their prosperity (of which the law, *nomos* or *themis*, is a guarantee)—becomes altered. And those who do write their laws, or who begin writing them at a later time, put them out for public display, to ensure not only that everyone knows them, but also that no one changes anything in them, not a single iota, because it is difficult to change what is written—in stone or bronze—when it is displayed in a public place.[41]

Oral or unwritten laws, on the contrary, are known to everyone who participates in social and political life. Such laws cannot be misapprehended or changed either intentionally or unintentionally by a single person or group, even if a group usurps power. Unwritten laws cannot be altered, and if they are modified, then the transformation occurs over time and reflects changes in communal and political life. In addition, unwritten laws are more easily adapted to new circumstances. The letter of an oral law, unlike that of a written law, can also more easily preserve the spirit of the law itself. On the contrary, a written law, because it is written, is stiff, inflexible, and "unmovable." Written law does not "talk back"—only its interpreters do—and preserves itself and its letter, which, with time, may come to be at odds with its spirit.

For this reason, Aristotle takes unwritten laws, which are based on custom, to be more reliable and more important than written laws. A good politician, then, is the one who acts as though "in between" the written and the unwritten or oral, being more efficient than an inflexible written law yet less reliable than the governing oral law.[42] A similar attitude to law is found in Thucydides, whose Pericles praises the Athenian democracy by stressing that its members obey the laws out of respect, not only the written laws that protect the citizens, but also the unwritten laws, the violation of which is considered an act of disgrace and turpitude.[43]

Unwritten laws are thus preferable to written ones. An unwritten law is oral, and if it is not always univocal in its formulation, it is still unambiguous in its meaning—that is, in evoking justice. Justice is exercised and restored anew each time through oral law even if justice might be elusive in its ultimate dialectical definition. Unwritten laws, then, ensure both the stability of a social and political community in the turmoil of public life and the just treatment of the members of a community. Insofar as unwritten law is flexible without being opportunistic, it allows for justice in cases that might not be foreseen by an existing written law. Because it needs to be reapplied in each concrete case in order to ensure justice, an unwritten law needs to be reinterpreted each time. In this sense, unwritten laws are dialogical because they require effort in order to be understood in discussion both with other members of the political community and with the tradition of their previous interpretation and application.

Written laws, on the contrary, are dialectical. They are represented in and as a fixed transcription of legal norms, which may not have to do with justice directly. Laws, on this account, coincide with a system of fixed written norms, so that each legal decision may be logically deduced from a closed system and be established solely within that system (as is the case with twentieth-century legal positivism, which is represented in Kelsen and Hart and is based on the tradition of Roman law). This is the idea of law that uses the grammar of logic and the procedures of dialectic.

An unwritten law always points as though beyond itself toward justice that transcends any finite legal norm. The source and origin of law that surpasses any written fixation is taken symbolically as divine. Such is also traditionally the figure of the lawgiver. Reportedly, Lycurgus gave laws to Sparta in the form of brief maxims that are oracular sayings brought from Delphi. Each saying, a so-called *rhētra*, establishes the divine authority of both the lawgiver and the laws, which are given by a deity in and as the oracle. (Stressing the divine origin of law might, of course, also be a trick of the lawgiver to secure due respect for the law.)[44] One of these maxims explicitly says that the law must remain unwritten. The reason for this is that, on the one hand, the cardinal laws are applied not so much through formal prescriptions as through morals that are built into social customs and habits and are based on free will, which is subject to training and education at a young age. On the other hand, the particular auxiliary laws that regulate the exchange of goods, pecuniary responsibilities, fines, and the like, are also better preserved in unwritten form because the social, economic, and political situation in which alone such laws are meaningful may in fact change in response to economic inflation, war, or other event. Therefore the current content of secondary social, economic, and political laws is better established by those who have knowledge and understanding of the corresponding matters (e.g., what the amount of a fine should be in a given case).[45] In all such instances the law is better off being unwritten because it is then preserved from corruption and better suited to concrete situations, while at the same time remaining common and universal. If the laws are written down, then they should be liberated from their condition of "writtenness" by the lawgiver in order to be restored to their full oral power. This is purportedly what Numa did when he stipulated that all the copies of his laws should be buried with him after his death.[46]

When Lycurgus established Spartan law, he wanted them to be preserved forever and kept intact as oral, and to that end he decided to deceive his fellow citizens for their own benefit. He said that he needed to leave again for Delphi to ask for an oracle from Apollo. Lycurgus asked the Spartans to swear under oath that they would not change anything in the laws until he returned, which they promised. However, in Delphi Lycurgus committed suicide, his body was burned, and his ashes, by preliminary arrangement, were scattered over the sea to make sure that his remains did not make it back to Sparta and that he never "returned."[47] Lycurgus thus gave up his life in order to secure the inviolability and unchangeability of the laws. Bound by their oath, the Spartans were obliged to keep the laws intact, the same laws that eventually created the Lacedemonian polis, one of the most powerful and politically influential in the ancient world, which seems to justify Lycurgus' self-sacrifice.

This pattern of self-sacrifice for the sake of preserving one's legacy in an inviolable and unwritten law is easily recognized in Socrates, who might have escaped death and execution.[48] Instead, he preferred to stay in prison in order to live life by leaving it, as is proper for a philosopher. Socrates chose to become and be Lycurgus,[49] so that his "law," that of oral and live dialogue, a seemingly elusive yet definite philosophical practice and discourse, would be passed on living and alive. Socrates did so with astonishing success, for we are still doing philosophy today, following Socrates' not firmly codified yet clearly established oral law.

(Dialectical) Conclusion

Since dialogue cannot be finalized, cannot be brought to a point where each participant will gain his or her definite identity and every notion will find its place within a univocally defined system, a conclusion to a book on dialogue and its relation to dialectic seems superfluous. Perhaps it is better to finish the discussion with a crafted dialectical argument about dialogue, which proceeds in an Aristotelian way, and, unlike dialogue, is both complete and completed.

Whether the dialogue is unfinalizable?

We proceed thus: *Objection 1*. It would seem that dialogue is finalizable insofar as a conversation should be complete and thus completed and final. Otherwise, if left unfinished, any speech would be without a conclusion and therefore without an end, and hence without meaning.

Objection 2. Furthermore, those involved in either a conversation or an argument have a finite capacity of reasoning. To prove a point, one needs to do so in a finite and definite number of steps. Therefore, for finite reason, unfinalizable reasoning is impossible.

Objection 3. Moreover, a dialogue must be finalizable because at a certain point all of the possible and discernible meanings of the notion or question being debated will be mentioned and sufficiently discussed, so there will be nothing left to say except as a repetition of what has already been said.

Objection 4. Finally, if it were unfinalizable, a dialogue would come to a standstill once the interlocutors (or one of them) do not want to continue, simply decide to stop, or find it impossible to continue the conversation.

On the contrary, as Socrates says (Plato, *Lysis* 222E): δέομαι . . . τὰ εἰρημένα ἄπαντα ἀναπεμπάσασθαι. ("I need . . . to rethink entirely what was said"), concerning which the gloss states: "dialogue always allows one to reconsider, together with the other and from a different perspective, what has already been said, and also to discuss something utterly novel within a new exchange."

I answer that it is not impossible that dialogue may be unfinalizable, and it is necessary for dialogue to continue further both about the same topic and about different ones. For dialogue is a decentered conversation, an exchange of rejoinders by multiple interlocutors in which each interlocutor is present as a uniquely recognizable and recognized voice, through which each one communicates with the others and expresses one's personal other. The driving force of dialogue is not the unity and struggle of contradictory opposites, but rather allosensus, a non-confrontational disagreement that allows one to listen to the other and to continue the discussion. The unfinalizability of dialogue lies in the impossibility of extinguishing one's personal other, and of fully and ultimately thematizing or framing oneself in a finite number of statements through discussion or the steps of an argument. Hence dialogue can always be continued and renewed without any repetition of its contents.

Reply to Objection 1. That dialogue is unfinalizable, that it can always be continued without exhaustion or repetition, does not mean that it is unfinished. Dialogue is meaningful at any point even if the discussion arrives at a perplexing impasse. The very attempt to understand one's own misunderstanding is fruitful, and a lack of meaning is meaningful insofar as it allows one to continue the discussion.

Reply to Objection 2. Certainly, to be complete and completed, an argument needs to be carried out in a finite number of steps. Yet dialogue is not about producing arguments, which, although they can be obtained within dialogue, are as though a by-product of dialogical discussion;

valid arguments can also be established in and by monological thinking. Dialogue concerns communication with the other and the expression of one's personal other, which is neither a thing, nor a notion, nor a function of social or historical arrangements. Human finitude is present precisely in and through an unfinalizable exchange with the other person, which always involves one's personal other that cannot be fully thematized or represented in any number of statements.

Reply to Objection 3. Again, a property of a thing or the meaning of a term may, but does not need to be, discussed in dialogue: they can equally both be considered in the absence of a real other who responds, interrupts, and disagrees. Furthermore, even in a discussion about a particular notion, nothing guarantees that the Prodican program of discerning all possible meanings can be realized because nothing prevents a new but not yet identified meaning from being discerned or produced within a new context or conversational situation, and nothing prevents the emergence of new usage for the term, or guarantees that within the already discussed and established meaning there is nothing left over for further subdivisions.

Reply to Objection 4. To be in dialogue is to communicate with other persons through an exchange of rejoinders in an interaction where each voice sounds independently but also within the whole of the dialogue, which in turn is irreducible to the sum of its constituents. Hence a single voice separate from others in dialogue is a *contradictio in adiecto.* Whoever chooses to stop dialogical conversation with others by an act of voluntary self-suspension chooses not to be, because to be is to be in dialogue.

Notes

1. "*[T]on hēttō . . . logon kreittō poiein*" (Protagoras, B6b DK [cit. ap. Aristotle, *Rhetoric* 1402a23]). Cf. *Dissoi Logoi* 1.1 sqq.

2. The term "dialectic" (*dialektikē* [sc. *tekhnē*]) appears to have been invented by Plato, as well as other terms ending in -*ikē*, such as "rhetoric" (*rhētorikē*), "eristic" (*eristikē*), and "disputation" (*antilogikē*). See E. Schiappa, *Protagoras and Logos: A Study in Greek Philosophy and Rhetoric* (Columbia: University of South Carolina Press, 1991), p. 44.

3. See Aristotle, *Peri tagathoy.*

4. Diogenes Laertius, III.18.

5. Diogenes Laertius, III.48.

6. The late *Anonymous Prolegomena to Platonic Philosophy* characterizes dialogue as a "discourse in prose [*logos aney metroy*, i.e., nonmetric] consisting of questions and answers by various persons, each properly characterized" (*Anonymous Prolegomena to Platonic Philosophy*, trans. L. G. Westerink [Amsterdam: North-Holland, 1962], IV.14, 3–5).

7. Plato, *Symposium* 185C–E.

8. Plato, *Phaedrus* 264C. According to the *Anonymous Prolegomena* (V.16–17), dialogue is cosmos and cosmos is dialogue: both have the same constituents (matter, form, nature, soul, intellect, and divinity), such that dialogue symbolically maps the living organism of the cosmos, where the whole and the parts fit with each other in such a way that one does not exist without the others. The matter of dialogue consists in its characters, its time, and its place; the form of dialogue is its style; its nature is the way in which the discussion is conducted; soul is its demonstration; intellect is the problem being discussed; and divinity is the good.

9. C. Kahn, "The Philosophical Importance of the Dialogue Form for Plato," *Graduate Faculty Philosophy Journal* 26:1 (2005), pp. 13–28.

10. See D. Nails, *The People of Plato: A Prosopography of Plato and Other Socratics* (Indianapolis: Hackett, 2002).

11. Plato, *Symposium* 215A–222A.

12. M. Frede, "Plato's Arguments and the Dialogue Form," *Oxford Studies in Ancient Philosophy, Supplementary Volume: Methods of Interpreting Plato and His Dialogues*, ed. J. C. Klagge and N. D. Smith (Oxford: Oxford University Press, 1992), pp. 201–219.

13. See, e.g., Plato, *Laches* 200E–201B; *Charmides* 175A–D; *Hippias Minor* 376B–C; *Lysis* 222B–223B. On the role of aporetic and paradoxical endings in Plato as a propaedeutic to philosophy and as hypomnematic (a reminder) used for educational purposes, see M. Erler, *Der Sinn der Aporien in den Dialogen Platons. Übungsstücke zur Anleitung im philosophischen Denken* (Berlin: De Gruyter, 1987), p. 280 sqq. et passim.

14. Plato, *Republic* 354C.

15. See, e.g., Plato, *Charmides* 175C–E; *Euthyphro* 15C–E; *Lysis* 223E.

16. *Anonymous Prolegomena* IV.15.

17. Aristotle, *Metaphysics* 987b32–33.

18. Plato, *Republic* 533C sqq.

19. See Plato, *Phaedrus* 261A sqq.

20. Plato, *Sophist* 230D.

21. Plato, *Euthydemus* 298A–C; 299D–E.

22. Cf. Parmenides, A28 DK I 223, 3–9 (ap. Simplicius, *In Phys.* 115.11 sqq.).

23. Aristotle, *Physics* 185a21 (*pollakhōs legetai to on*); *Metaphysics* 1003a33 (*to de on legetai men pollakhōs*).

24. Aristotle, *Metaphysics* 1014b16–1015a19; 1017a7–1017b26. Cf. F. Brentano, *On the Several Senses of Being in Aristotle*, trans. and ed. Rolf George (Berkeley: University of California Press, 1975).

25. See, e.g., Plato, *Charmides* 163D; *Cratylus* 384B; also Prodicus, A11, A13–A20 DK. Cf. Alcinous, *Didaskalikos* 6.11: the correct use of names belongs to dialectic.

26. Aristotle, *Topica* 112b22 sqq. Cf. Plato, *Euthydemus* 277E; *Protagoras* 337C; *Meno* 75E.

CHAPTER 2

1. Diogenes Laertius, III.48. Cf. Plato, *Cratylus* 390C.

2. Plato, *Meno* 73D sqq.; *Republic* 453A–C. Cf. *Anonymous Prolegomena* IV.15.

3. See, e.g., Plato, *Republic* 511A–E.

4. Plato, *Meno* 75D; cf. *Gorgias* 472B–C.

5. Proclus, *In Primum Euclidis Elementorum Librum Commentarii*, ed. G. Friedlein (Leipzig: Teubner, 1873), 44.14–24.

6. Galileo Galilei, *Dialogue Concerning Two Chief World Systems: Ptolemaic and Copernican*, trans. S. Drake (New York: Modern Library, 2001), p. 119.

7. Proclus, *In Euclidem* 44.2–3. Cf. Iamblichus, *De communi mathematica scientia*, ed. N. Festa and U. Klein (Munich: K. G. Saur Verlag, 1998), 89.16–90.27.

8. Plato, *Republic* 511B–D; 533D–534A; 537C.

9. Plato, *Phaedrus* 276E–277A; *Euthydemus* 292C.

10. Plato, *Republic* 509B; cf. 533C–D; 534B–C.

11. Plato, *Republic* 531C–535A; cf. *Euthydemus* 290C; *Philebus* 57E–58A. Reflections on dialectic belong to the later Platonic dialogues, although in the *Laws* the notion of dialectic is mentioned only briefly. See *Laws* 286A, 286E–287A.

12. Thus Herbart takes method to be a universal way of deducing something from principles. J. F. Herbart, *Lehrbuch zur Einleitung in die Philosophie*, ed. W. Henckmann (Hamburg: Meiner, 1993), p. 58.

13. Plato, *Sophist* 253D–E.

14. Cf. Iamblichus, *De communi mathematica scientia*, 65.15–20. Alcinous distinguishes three different kinds of collection (which he calls *analysis*): "the first is an ascent from sense-objects to the primary intelligibles; the second is an ascent through what can be demonstrated and indicated to propositions which are indemonstrable and immediate; and third is that which advances upwards from a hypothesis to non-hypothetical first principles" (Alcinous, *Didaskalikos* 5.4–6). The second kind of analysis can be useful in both philosophical (cf. Plato, *Phaedrus* 245C–246A) and mathematical proofs: given the premises, and the conclusion yet to be proven, one assumes the conclusion as hypothetical and then attempts to show that the premises can be reached "backwards"—this is analysis proper. If the connection between the conclusion and the premises can be established in this way, then one has to move in the opposite direction, this time from the premises to the conclusion, thereby reversing the procedure—this is "synthesis." Analysis and synthesis are thus mutually connected, and if the two can be consecutively performed, then the proposition in question is considered established and justified.

15. Plato, *Phaedrus* 265C–266C; *Sophist* 253D–E; *Statesman* 259D–267C, 276C–292C. Cf. Plotinus, *Enneads* I.3.4.13–16. Aristotle, who devotes a great deal of attention to elaborating the method of analysis, criticizes Platonic "division," which for Aristotle can be practiced only under certain restrictions because it is not capable of properly demonstrating that the subject being considered has the exact attributes that are ascribed to it. See Aristotle, *Analytica Priora* 46a32 sqq.; *Analytica Posteriora* 91b13 sqq., 96a25 sqq.

16. Cf. Plato, *Philebus* 16C–18D.

17. Aristotle, *Analytica posteriora* 71a5–11. Cf. Alcinous, *Didaskalikos* 3.2, 5.1–6.4. The five parts of dialectic—division, definition, analysis, induction, and syllogistic—became commonly accepted in later philosophy. See J. Dillon in Alcinous, *The Handbook of Platonism* (Oxford: Oxford University Press, 1993), pp. 72–77. Proclus, however, mentions four methods of dialectic: analysis, division/diairesis,

definition, and demonstration (*In Euclidem* 42.19–43.10; 69.13–19). In his commentary on Plato's *Parmenides*, Proclus also excludes the Aristotelian procedure of induction (*Commentarium in Platonis Parmenidem* 796.16–26; 980.17 sqq). Cf. also *Anonymous Prolegomena* XI.27, where fifteen ways of dialogical instruction are enumerated, including all of the five parts or particular methods that pertain to dialectic.

18. Gaiser distinguishes six methods (species, *eidē*) or ways (*hodoi*) of dialectic, some of which are mutually implied (cf. Plato, *Republic* 532E): (1) *elenxis* or *elenchus*; (2) *diairesis* and *synagōgē*; (3) *analysis* and *synthesis*; (4) *mesotēs* (*Statesman* 283C–285C), identifying a middle or "excellence" (*aretē*) as a measure and middle between the extremes of more and less, too much and too little; (5) *hypothesis*, finding hypothetical causal connections between the most general causes and phenomena (cf. Plato, *Parmenides* 137C sqq.); and (6) *mimēsis*, the study of correspondences between, and deviations from, one presupposed paradigm and its many imitations (K. Gaiser, "Platonische Dialektik—damals und heute," in *Gesammelte Schriften*, ed. T. A. Szlezák und K.-H. Stanzel [St. Augustin: Academia, 2004], pp. 177–203). One might also add to these the mentioned method of distinguishing names, which is intended as a way of avoiding ambiguity.

19. Alcinous, *Didaskalikos* 3.1: dialectic is one of the three constituent parts of philosophy, along with theoretical and practical philosophy. As the knowledge of *reason*, however, dialectic does not itself belong either to theoretical philosophy (which studies "what is") or to practical philosophy (which studies "what is to be done"). This classification followed Xenocrates' (frag. 1, ed. Heinze) division of philosophy into physics, ethics, and logic, which was also later used by the Stoics. If dialectic is neither theoretical nor practical, then it is the knowledge of the pure forms of reasoning that allows one to know "the meaning of speech," as Alcinous says, i.e., *logos*, or the essence and definition of each thing.

20. Aristotle, *Metaphysics* 1026a6–22. Cf. Plato, *Republic* 521D sqq. and Proclus' classification of the four sciences of the quadrivium (*In Euclidem* 35.21–36.7).

21. Proclus, *In Euclidem* 42.9–19.

22. Plato, *Republic* 511C (the simile of the line); cf. Alcinous, *Didaskalikos* 7.5.

23. See, e.g., R. Descartes, *Regulae*, vol. 10 of *Oeuvres*, ed. C. Adam and P. Tannery (Paris: Cerf, 1897–1913), IV, p. 376 sqq.; and *Discourse*, vol. 6 of *Oeuvres*, III, p. 29 sqq.

24. Plato, *Meno* 80A–E.

25. Plato, *Phaedrus* 276E. According to Diogenes Laertius, "Dialectic is the art of speeches or arguments (*tekhnē logōn*)" (Diogenes Laertius, III.48).

26. Aristotle, *Physics* 194a21–22, 194b1–2, 199a15–17.

27. Pliny, *Historia naturalis* XXXV.65–66.

28. See D. Nikulin, *Matter, Imagination and Geometry: Ontology, Natural Philosophy and Mathematics in Plotinus, Proclus and Descartes* (Aldershot, UK: Ashgate, 2002), p. 132 sqq.

29. Plato, *Euthydemus* 291B.

30. Aristotle, *Analytica Priora* 46a9; *Analytica Posteriora* 81a18–20; *Topica* 100b18; *Sophistici elenchi* 183a34 sqq. A syllogism (*syllogismos*) is a speech or argument (*logos*) from which, if something is presupposed, something *different* must necessarily follow (*Topica* 100b25 sqq.); and a premise is "a speech that affirms or negates something about something" (*Analytica Priora* 24a22 sqq.). In the *Topics*, Aristotle investigates the common places, *topoi*, of arguing, with reference to particular kinds of problems by means of a dialectical syllogism (*Topica* 101a25 sqq.). The dialecticians, according to Aristotle, attempt to inquire about the same and the other, the similar and the dissimilar, the opposite, the prior and the posterior, and all other such things by starting from probable contentions only (*Metaphysics* 995b21–24). These "probable contentions," which define the dialectical or epicheirematic syllogism, are based on the so-called *endoxa*, which denote "whatever you can get your opponent to agree to, i.e., based on reputable opinions, which he might be expected to accept" (Dillon, commentary on Alcinous, *The Handbook of Platonism*, p. 59); *endoxa* can thus be considered "thèses probables" (P. Aubenque, *Le problème de l'être chez Aristote* [Paris: Presses Universitaires de France, 1966], pp. 258–259).

31. Aristotle, *Topica* 100b23. See also the anonymous *Dissoi Logoi*.

32. See Aristotle, *Topica* 104b1 sqq. Every Platonic dialogue can be represented as a dialectical syllogism (argument) defined by the following five components: (1) the main problem; (2) the four ways or means of constructing a syllogism ("instruments" or "tools," *organa*); (3) a set of rules for providing the conclusion; (4) the strategy of the questioner; and (5) the strategy of the responder. The *organa* are: (i) choosing the correct assumptions and premises and constructing more specific ones by dividing the terms; (ii) distinguishing the different meanings of a word; (iii) finding distinctions within one and the same genus or within close genera; and (iv) finding similarities between objects of different genera and identity within objects of the same genus. The set of all possible dialectical arguments with the different components listed above should then coincide with the set of formal structures of all possible (written and unwritten) dialogues (*Topica* 105b34 sqq.). See also the commentary of Z. Mikeladze in vol. 2 of Aristotle, *Sochineniya* (Moscow: Mysl', 1978), pp. 595–596.

33. Aristotle, *Metaphysics* 1004b17–26; cf. *Topica* 155b7–15.

34. Aristotle, *Analytica Posteriora* 74b10–11; *Topica* 162a15–18; cf. *Sophistici elenchi* 165b1–9. A dialectical conclusion differs from an eristic one in that the eristic conclusion is based solely on premises that only *seem* to be probable and plausible but in reality are not. The purpose of the eristic conclusion, however, is to profit and gain by winning a dispute through any means. Aristotle, *Sophistici elenchi* 183a34 sqq.; cf. 164a37 sqq. and 171b25–27. In *Topica* 101a1–4, Aristotle further suggests distinguishing between the eristic and the sophistic syllogism: whereas the

former makes the correct conclusion from premises that only seem to be plausible, the latter does so incorrectly.

35. Aristotle, *Metaphysics* 1061b7–10; *Topica* 105b30–31. Only *nous*, being the identity of thinking and the object of thought, is capable of immediately grasping the validity of the first and unprovable principles of knowledge or *epistēmē*. Aristotle, *Analytica Posteriora* 88b35 sqq., 100b5–17. Cf. Thomas Aquinas, *In libros Posteriorum analyticorum Aristotelis expositio* I, XV, 133.

36. To be precise, Aristotle makes a further distinction between a dialectical problem and a dialectical statement or premise (*protasis*) according to the way in which each one is expressed: in the dialectical problem, both alternatives being referred to are present by being explicitly formulated, whereas in the dialectical statement only one of the premises is mentioned, while the other is only meant or presupposed. Aristotle, *Topica* 101b28 sqq.; 104b1 sqq.; 158a15–17.

37. Plato, *Phaedrus* 266D sqq.

38. Another "instrument" for persuasion according to Aristotle is the use of example in induction. Aristotle, *Rhetoric* 1355a2 sqq.; *Analytica Priora* 70a10 sqq.; *Analytica Posteriora* 71a9–10.

39. Aristotle, *Metaphysics* 1004b20; *Topica* 101a36 sqq.; cf. *Analytica Posteriora* 77a27 sqq. and *Sophistici elenchi* 170a38–39.

40. Aristotle, *Sophistici elenchi* 172a12 sqq.

41. Cf. Xenocrates, frag. 1, ed. Heinze; and Alcinous, *Didaskalikos* 3.1.

42. Cf. Armstrong's note in Plotinus, *Enneads*, trans. and ed. A. H. Armstrong, vol. 1 (Cambridge, Mass.: Harvard University Press, 1966), I.3.4, pp. 158–159n2.

43. See *Die Fragmente zur Dialektik der Stoiker. Neue Sammlung der Texte mit deutscher Übersetzung und Kommentar*, ed. K. Hülser, 4 vols. (Stuttgart/Bad Cannstatt: Frommann-Holzboog, 1987–1988), vol. 1, pp. 2–246.

44. Diogenes Laertius, VII.43–83. See also B. Mates, *Stoic Logic* (Berkeley: University of California Press, 1961).

45. Plotinus, *Enneads* I.3.4.1–9.

46. Plotinus, *Enneads* I.3.1.1–5; I.3.1.16–17; I.3.4.15–20; I.3.5.8–10; I.3.5.17–19; I.3.6. Plato, *Republic* 532E.

CHAPTER 3

1. Immanuel Kant, *Kritik der reinen Vernunft* (KrV), in *Werkausgabe*, vols. 3–4, ed. Wilhelm Weischedel (Frankfurt am Main: Suhrkamp, 1974), B85 sqq.; B349–356; B378; B390. The three ideas of pure reason in Kant—souls, world, and God—are removed from reality because they cannot be found in any possible experience or in any phenomenon *in concreto* (KrV B595), which makes the three corresponding disciplines, *psychologia rationalis*, *cosmologia rationalis*, and *theologia transcendentalis* (KrV B391–392), into pseudo-sciences insofar as they are based

on speculative principles that need to be criticized for the illusoriness of their conclusions (in the paralogisms, antinomies, and proofs).

2. On the distinction between logical (or analytic), dialectical (further distinguished into contrary and subcontrary), and real opposition in Kant, see M.
Wolff, *Der Begriff des Widerspruchs. Eine Studie zur Dialektik Kants und Hegels*
(Königstein: Hain, 1981), pp. 41–77. Only logical opposition implies a contradiction, namely, when something is affirmed and denied of the same thing at the
same time (KrV B190–191; B320–321; B531; cf. B489). Real opposition arises when
two predicates of the same thing are opposed without contradiction. Cf. I. Kant,
"Versuch, den Begriff der negativen Größen in die Weltweisheit einzuführen," in
vol. 2 of *Werkausgabe*, p. 783.

3. Nicholas of Cusa, *De docta ignorantia,* I.2.5; I.22.69 et passim.

4. Aristotle, *Metaphysics* 1005b19–20.

5. Plotinus, *Enneads* V.8.4.9. See also J. Halfwassen, *Plotin und der Neopla-
tonismus* (Munich: Beck, 2004), pp. 77–79.

6. Aristotle, *Analytica Posteriora* 72a12–14; *Categories* 13b36–14a25; cf. *Physics*
189a35 sqq. and Plato, *Phaedo* 103C–E.

7. Aristotle, *Metaphysics* 1046b22–24, 1051a10–12.

8. Diogenes Laertius, III.35.

9. G. W. F. Hegel, *Wissenschaft der Logik*, in vol. 5 of *Werke* (Frankfurt am
Main: Suhrkamp, 1986), pp. 82–83.

10. G. W. F. Hegel, *Enzyklopädie der philosophischen Wissenschaften in
Grundrisse. Erster Teil: Die Wissenschaft der Logik*, in vol. 8 of *Werke*, §§79–82, pp.
168–179.

11. Cf. G. W. F. Hegel, *Vorlesungen über die Geschichte der Philosophie*, in vol. 19
of *Werke*, p. 62. "Dialektik aber nennen wir die höhere vernünftige Bewegung, in
welche solche schlechthin getrennt Scheinende durch sich selbst, durch das, was sie
sind, ineinander übergehen, die Voraussetzung [ihrer Getrenntheit] sich aufhebt"
(Hegel, *Wissenschaft der Logik*, p. 111); "We call dialectic the higher movement of reason in which such seemingly utterly separate terms pass over into each other spon-
taneously, through that which they are, a movement in the presupposition sublates
itself" (G. W. F. Hegel, *Science of Logic*, trans. A. V. Miller [London: Allen & Unwin,
1969], p. 105). See also G. W. F. Hegel, *Grundlinien der Philosophie des Rechts*, in vol.
7 of *Werke*, §31, p. 84. Notably, Hegel's first habilitation thesis runs: "Contradictio
est regula veri, non contradictio falsi" (in vol. 2 of *Werke*, p. 533).

12. Cf. Adorno's critique in T. W. Adorno, *Negative Dialectics*, trans. E. B. Ash-
ton (New York: Continuum, 1973), pp. 161–162. On Nietzsche's critique of dialectic, see G. Deleuze, *Nietzsche and Philosophy*, trans. H. Tomlinson (New York:
Columbia University Press, 2006), p. 147 sqq.

13. One might make a further distinction between concepts and conceptions:
concepts (which are nonexplanatory and are expressed by a term) are eventually

defined within a determinate and finalized system of conceptions (which are ex-planatory and are expressed by a proposition). See T. Pinkard, *Hegel's Dialectic: The Explanation of Possibility* (Philadelphia: Temple University Press, 1988), pp. 13–14.

14. "Non-being belongs to being, it cannot be separated from it. We could not even think 'being' without a double negation: being must be thought as the negation of the negation of being" (P. Tillich, *The Courage to Be* [New Haven, Conn.: Yale University Press, 1952], p. 179).

15. K. Popper, "What Is Dialectic?" in *Conjectures and Refutations: The Growth of Scientific Knowledge*, 2nd ed. (New York: Harper & Row, 1965), pp. 312–35. (In-deed, if p and -p is assumed, then p; p v q; -p; ergo, q for any q whatsoever.)

16. "[D]ie Tätigkeit des Sich-selbst-Denkens in sich selbst" (Hegel, *Vorlesungen über die Geschichte der Philosophie II*, in vol. 19 of *Werke*, p. 82).

17. See ibid., pp. 74–75: "Die höchste Form bei Platon ist die Identität des Seins und Nichtsein [The highest form in Plato is the identity of being and non-being]."

18. Ibid., pp. 62–86.

19. E.g., J. Derrida, *Of Grammatology*, trans. Gayatri V. Spivak (Baltimore: Johns Hopkins University Press, 1974), p. 143. Cf.: "Nontruth is the truth. Non-presence is presence. Differance, the disappearance of any originary presence, is *at once* the condition of possibility *and* the condition of impossibility of truth" (J. Derrida, "Plato's Pharmacy," in *Dissemination*, trans. B. Johnson [Chicago: University of Chicago Press, 1981], pp. 63–171, 168–169).

20. C. Taylor, "Dialektik heute, oder: Strukturen der Selbstnegation," in D. Henrich, ed., *Hegels Wissenschaft der Logik. Formation und Rekonstruktion* (Stuttgart: Klett-Cotta, 1986), pp. 141–153. See also R. B. Pippin, *Hegel's Idealism: The Satisfactions of Self-Consciousness* (Cambridge: Cambridge University Press, 1989), p. 308.

21. "[K]onkrete Vorstellungen, nicht reine Gedanken" (Hegel, *Vorlesungen über die Geschichte der Philosophie II*, p. 69).

22. G. W. F. Hegel, *Vorlesungen über die Ästhetik*, in vol. 15 of *Werke*, p. 493.

23. Hegel, *Vorlesungen über die Geschichte der Philosophie II*, pp. 21, 26 sqq., 68–69.

24. G. W. F. Hegel, *Berliner Schriften*, in vol. 11 of *Werke*, p. 268. See K. W. F. Solger, *Erwin: Vier Gespräche über das Schöne und die Kunst* (Berlin, 1815), pts. 1–2.

25. F. D. E. Schleiermacher, *Dialektik (1814/15)/Einleitung zur Dialektik (1833)*, ed. A. Arndt (Hamburg: Meiner, 1988), pp. 3, 7, et al. See also M. Frank, *Das individuelle Allgemeine. Textstrukturierung und -interpretation nach Schleiermacher* (Frankfurt am Main: Suhrkamp, 1985), pp. 121–33.

26. Schleiermacher, *Dialektik*, pp. 8–9. Cf. *Einleitung zur Dialektik*, pp. 115–16.

27. In Gadamer's formulation, "das Gespräch ist nichts als die wechselseitige Anregung der Gedankenerzeugung" (H.-G. Gadamer, *Wahrheit und Methode: Grundzüge einer philosophischen Hermeneutik*, vol. 1 of *Gesammelte Werke* [Tübingen: J. C. B. Mohr, 1990], p. 192); "Dialogue is nothing but the mutual stimulation of thought" (*Truth and Method*, trans. J. Weinsheimer and D. G. Marshall, rev. ed. [London: Continuum, 2004], p. 187).

28. "Dialektik ist Darlegung der Grundsätze für die kunstmäßige Gesprächführung im Gebiet des reinen Denkens" (Schleiermacher, *Einleitung zur Dialektik*, p. 117 sqq.). Cf. also M. Frank, "Einleitung des Herausgebers," in Schleiermacher, vol. 1 of *Dialektik* (Frankfurt am Main: Suhrkamp, 2001), p. 10 sqq.

29. "Die Dialektik ist kein Monolog der Spekulation mit sich selbst, sondern ein Dialog der Spekulation und Empirie" (L. Feuerbach, *Kleinere Schriften II (1839–1846)*, vol. 9 of *Gesammelte Werke*, ed. W. Schuffenhauer [Berlin: Akadamie Verlag, 1970], p. 37).

30. F. D. E. Schleiermacher, *Hermeneutik*, ed. H. Kimmerle (Heidelberg: Carl Winter, 1959). Cf. Gadamer, *Wahrheit und Methode*, pp. 188–201; and A. Bowie, "Introduction," in F. D. E. Schleiermacher, *Hermeneutics and Criticism*, trans. and ed. A. Bowie (Cambridge: Cambridge University Press, 1998), pp. xix–xxvi.

31. Gadamer, *Wahrheit und Methode*, p. 368 sqq.

32. H.-G. Gadamer, *The Idea of the Good in Platonic-Aristotelian Philosophy*, trans. P. Christopher Smith (New Haven, Conn.: Yale University Press, 1986), pp. 104–125, esp. 109.

33. H.-G. Gadamer, *Dialogue and Dialectic: Eight Hermeneutical Studies on Plato*, trans. P. Christopher Smith (New Haven, Conn.: Yale University Press, 1980), pp. 93–123, 122; italics added. Cf. H.-G. Gadamer, *Platons dialektische Ethik und andere Studien zur platonischen Philosophie* (Hamburg: Meiner, 1968), pp. 52–80, 89–100.

34. Gadamer, *Wahrheit und Methode*, pp. 372–374.

CHAPTER 4

1. D. Nikulin, *On Dialogue* (Lanham, Md.: Lexington Books, 2006). For a more detailed discussion of the personal other (as "eidema"), see idem, pp. 69–97.

2. See Marcel van Ackeren, "Die Philosophie Marc Aurels: Beobachtungen zu Form und Inhalt der *Selbstbetrachtungen*," Habilitationsschrift, University of Cologne, 2009.

3. Unlike Sartre's "*l'homme se fait.*" J.-P. Sartre, *L'existentialisme est un humanisme* (1946; repr. Paris: Nagel, 1966), p. 78.

4. Cf. J. Habermas, *On the Pragmatics of Social Interaction: Preliminary Studies in the Theory of Communicative Action*, trans. Barbara Fultner (Cambridge: Polity Press, 2001), p. 89 sqq. et passim; and also: "[D]ebate constitutes the very essence

of political life" (H. Arendt, "Truth and Politics," in *Between Past and Future* [New York: Viking Press, 1961], p. 241).

5. D. Nikulin, "Dialogue versus Discourse: On the Possibility of Disagreement in Human Communication," *Graduate Faculty Philosophy Journal* 26:1 (2005), pp. 89–105.

6. Cf. M. Bakhtin, *Problems of Dostoevsky's Poetics*, ed. and trans. C. Emerson (Minneapolis: University of Minnesota Press, 1984), pp. 17 sqq.

7. C. Taylor, "The Dialogical Self," in *The Interpretive Turn: Philosophy, Science, Culture*, ed. R. Hiley et al. (Ithaca, N.Y.: Cornell University Press, 1991), p. 311.

8. Cf. Euripides, *Bacchae* 1288 sqq.

9. R. Descartes, *Meditations III*, in vol. 7 of *Oeuvres*, pp. 34 sqq. et passim.

10. M. Bakhtin, vol. 5 of *Sobranie sochineniy* (Moscow: Russkie slovari, 1996), pp. 325, 350, 367.

11. Plato, *Gorgias* 449B–C.

12. Herodotus, *Histories* III.46.

13. See Charles Perrault's dialogues: *Parallèle des anciens et des modernes en ce qui regarde les arts et les sciences*, ed. H. R. Jauss (Munich: Eidos Verlag, 1964).

14. For a discussion of dialogue as a philosophical genre, see V. Hösle, *Der philosophische Dialog. Eine Poetik und Hermeneutik* (Munich: C. H. Beck, 2006).

CHAPTER 5

1. L. P. Yakubinsky, "On Dialogic Speech," *Proceedings of the Modern Language Association of America* 112:2 (1997), pp. 243–256. The article was first published in 1923. In this chapter, Yakubinsky's article is quoted by reference to page number. See also V. Erlich, *Russian Formalism: History–Doctrine* (The Hague: Mouton, 1980), p. 237 et passim.

2. D. Nikulin, *On Dialogue*, pp. 231 sqq.

3. See M. Foucault, *Fearless Speech*, ed. Joseph Pearson (Los Angeles: Semiotext(e), 2001), pp. 115–133; and D. Nikulin, "Richard Rorty, Cynic: Philosophy in the Conversation of Humankind," *Graduate Faculty Philosophy Journal* 29:2 (2008), pp. 85–111.

4. E.g., Thucydides, V.85.

5. Plato, *Gorgias* 449B–C.

6. Dialogue "does not promote speech as a complex intentional activity grounded in deliberation, evaluation, and careful selection [of words and expressions]; on the contrary, it promotes speech as a simple volitional [i.e., directed at the 'what' rather than the 'how'–DN] activity using familiar elements" (Yakubinsky, "On Dialogic Speech," p. 251). As Yakubinsky notes, if for some reason the

interlocutor speaks slowly, "we are irritated and disturbed and consider delay inappropriate" (ibid.).

7. *A Greek-English Lexicon*, compiled by H. G. Liddell and R. Scott, 9th ed. (Oxford: Clarendon Press, 1940).

8. Cf. Protagoras, frag. B6a DK.

9. S. Beckett, *Waiting for Godot* (New York: Grove Press, 1982). All references are to page numbers in this edition.

CHAPTER 6

1. E. A. Havelock, *Origins of Western Literacy* (Toronto: Ontario Institute for Studies in Education, 1976); and E. A. Havelock, *The Muse Learns to Write: Reflections on Orality and Literacy from Antiquity to the Present* (New Haven, Conn.: Yale University Press, 1986).

2. Plato, *Phaedrus* 274B–277A.

3. Plato, *Hippias Major* 287B sqq.; *Crito* 50A–54D.

4. Plato, *Phaedrus* 274C–D. Cf. J. Assmann, *The Mind of Egypt: History and Meaning in the Time of the Pharaohs* (New York: Metropolitan Books, 2002), pp. 301–302.

5. "*[M]nēmēs te . . . kai sophias pharmakon*" (Plato, *Phaedrus* 274E). Plato is playing with the plurivocity of *pharmakon*, which may mean "cure" and "remedy" but also "poison," as well as "spell" and "enchanted potion" (see *A Greek-English Lexicon*).

6. See Plato, *Phaedrus* 275A–B.

7. Plato, *Phaedrus* 275A–E; cf. Plato, *Ion*.

8. See Hermias, *In Phaedrum* 258, 8–20.

9. Plato, *Phaedrus* 276A.

10. J. de Maistre, *Les soirées de Saint-Pétersbourg, ou entretiens sur le gouvernement de la Providence*, T. 1-2 (Paris, s. d. 1821), pt. 2, pp. 73, 76.

11. H.-G. Gadamer, "Mythos und Vernunft," in *Ästhetik und Poetik: Kunst als Aussage, Gesammelte Werke*, vol. 8 (Tübingen: Mohr, 1993), pp. 164–169.

12. Plato, *Phaedo* 89C–D.

13. P. Ricoeur, "Speaking and Writing," in *Interpretation Theory: Discourse and the Surplus of Meaning* (Fort Worth: Texas Christian University Press, 1976), p. 26.

14. Ibid., p. 43.

15. Ibid., p. 29.

16. Plato, *Epistola* VII, 342E–343A.

17. Plato, *Phaedrus* 275D–E.

18. *Anonymous Prolegomena* III.13: "Plato himself in the *Phaedrus* . . . criticizes writers of books because their writings [*syggrammata*], being lifeless, cannot defend themselves when doubts are raised, as they always say the same thing and

cannot answer a difficulty brought against them; therefore, he says, we should not write books, but leave pupils, who are living books [*empsykha syggrammata*]. This was also the practice of his predecessors: thus Socrates and Pythagoras left only pupils, not writings" (trans. Westerink; translation modified).

19. Ibid.

20. See W. J. Ong, *Orality and Literacy: The Technologizing of the Word* (1982; repr. London: Routledge, 1988), pp. 82–94 et passim.

21. For this reason, Plotinus puts Egyptian hieroglyphic writing above Greek phonetic writing (Plotinus, *Enneads* V.8.6).

22. Y. Olesha, *Envy, and Other Works*, trans. A. R. MacAndrew (Garden City, N.Y.: Doubleday, 1967), p. 4.

23. Plato, *Phaedrus* 276D.

24. H.-G. Gadamer, *Wahrheit und Methode. Grundzüge einer philosophischen Hermeneutik*, vol. 1 of *Gesammelte Werke* (Tübingen: J. C. B. Mohr, 1990), pp. 195–197; *Truth and Method*, trans. J. Weinsheimer and D. G. Marshall, rev. ed. (London: Continuum, 2004), pp. 190–192.

25. L. Strauss, *Persecution and the Art of Writing* (Chicago: University of Chicago Press, 1988), p. 8.

26. Ibid., pp. 25, 36.

27. Plato, *Phaedrus* 275B; Protagoras, B6 DK (ap. Aristotle, *Rhetoric* 1402a24).

28. Plutarch, *De defectu oraculorum*. Already Cicero says that the oracle at Delphi has long ago ceased to exist (*Divinatio Caecilum* 2). See also Plutarch, *De E apud Delphos*, and the dialogue *De Pythiae oraculis*.

29. Alcidamas, *Peri sophiston* 27–28, in Antiphon, *Orationes et fragmenta, adiunctis Gorgiae Antisthenis Alcidamantis declamationibus*, ed. F. Blass (Leipzig: Teubner, 1908), pp. 202–204; and Alcidamas, "On Those Who Write Written Speeches, or On Sophists," in Alcidamas, *The Works and Fragments*, ed. and trans. J. V. Muir (London: Bristol Classical Press, 2001), pp. 2–21. There is also a similarity in the defense of oral speech against writing between Plato's *Phaedrus* and Isocrates' *First Letter to Dionysius*. See L. Robin, commentary on the *Phaedrus* in vol. 4 of Platon, *Oeuvres complètes* (Paris: Pléiade, 1966), p. clxvi. The utter incapacity of lifeless letters to hold the live spirit of oral prescriptions is also ascribed to the Pythagoreans and to Numa by Plutarch, *Numa* 22, 1–8.

30. Gadamer takes Plato's criticism of "writtenness" (*Schriftlichkeit*) as an attempt to answer the Sophists' interpretations of texts at the time when philosophy and poetry turn into literature, and also as an attempt to overcome the weakness of sophistic *logoi*, thereby bringing language back to the original movement of live speech in Plato's own dialogical literary work (*Wahrheit und Methode*, p. 374; *Truth and Method*, pp. 362–363). This, however, would make Plato overcome one kind of writing, namely Sophistic written speeches, with yet another type of writing still unsuitable for transmitting and embracing oral speech.

31. Plato, *Epistola* VII, 341B–343A.

32. Aristotle, *Metaphysics* 987a29 sqq. Cf. G. W. F. Hegel, *Vorlesungen über die Geschichte der Philosophie*, in vol. 19 of *Werke*, p. 69. After Plato, Carneades does not write either, although for a different reason: being a skeptic, he denies any possibility of firm or sure knowledge, which makes its written presentation meaningless. Paradoxically, his successor and disciple Clitomachus was already a prolific writer, who in his writings preserved and tried to elucidate the arguments of Carneades (Diogenes Laertius, IV.65, 67).

33. Plato, *Phaedrus* 276C.

34. "[W]e undertake the writing of speeches both because we are eager to leave behind memorials [*mnēmeia*] of ourselves and to gratify our ambition [*philotimia*]" (Alcidamas, *Peri Sophiston* 32; see also 19–20, 31). Cf. Epictetus, *Discourses* I 19, 26–29.

35. Galileo Galilei, *Dialogue Concerning Two Chief World Systems*, pp. 120–121.

36. Aristotle, *Poetica* 1451b4–7.

37. Aristotle, *Politica* 1339a16. Cf. Euripides, frag. 856, ed. Nauck: "I play [amuse myself], for I always like to alternate labors [with delight]," and Thucydides, II.38,1.

38. Cf. *parergon* as *Zutat* in Immanuel Kant, *Kritik der Urteilskraft* B43.

39. "[A]*ei athanaton parekhein*" (Plato, *Phaedrus* 277A).

40. H. Westermann, *Die Intention des Dichters und die Zwecke der Interpreten: Zu Theorie und Praxis der Dichterauslegung in den platonischen Dialogen* (Berlin: De Gruyter, 2002), pp. 9–15.

41. See the preserved laws of the Cretan city of Gortyn from the late archaic to early classical periods: *The Law Code of Gortyn*, trans. and ed. R. F. Willetts (Berlin: De Gruyter, 1967). Cf. Plato, *Hippias Major* 284B.

42. Aristotle, *Politica* 1287b. Cf. also *Rhetorica* 1374a.

43. Thucydides, II.37, 3.

44. Plato, *Laws* 632D; Plutarch, *Lycurgus* 6, 1–10; cf. Plutarch, *Numa* 4, 12. See also Herodotus, *Histories* I.65–66.

45. Plutarch, *Lycurgus* 13, 1–4.

46. Plutarch, *Numa* 22, 2.

47. Plutarch, *Lycurgus* 29, 1–11; cf. 31, 1.

48. Plato, *Phaedo* 57A–64B; 115A–118A.

49. Socrates explicitly compares himself with Lycurgus, although Socrates stresses that he himself is only a human, whereas Lycurgus is greeted as a god by the oracle. Xenophon, *Apology* 15–16. Cf. Plato, *Phaedrus* 258C; *Republic* 599D.